The Journal of Andrew Fuller Studies

Published in the United States of America by
by The Andrew Fuller Center for Baptist Studies
The Southern Baptist Theological Seminary
2825 Lexington Road
Louisville, Kentucky 40280

© The Andrew Fuller Center for Baptist Studies 2021

All rights reserved. No part of this publication may be reproduced, stored in a retrieval system, or transmitted, in any form or by any means, without the prior permission in writing of The Andrew Fuller Center for Baptist Studies, or as expressly permitted by law, by license, or under terms agreed with the appropriate reproduction rights organization.

ISBN 978-1-77484-003-0

Printed by H&E Publishing, Peterborough, Ontario, Canada

The Journal for Andrew Fuller Studies

The *Journal of Andrew Fuller Studies* is an open access, double-blind peer-reviewed, scholarly journal published online biannually in February and September by the Andrew Fuller Center for Baptist Studies (under the auspices of The Southern Baptist Theological Seminary). The publication language of the journal is English. Articles that deal with the life, ministry, and thought of the Baptist pastor-theologian Andrew Fuller are very welcome, as well as essays on his friends, his Particular Baptist community in the long eighteenth century (1680s–1830s), and the global impact of his thought, known as "Fullerism."

Articles and book reviews are to follow generally the style of Kate L. Turabian, *A Manual for Writers of Research Papers, Theses, and Dissertations*, 9th ed. (Chicago: University of Chicago Press, 2018). They may be submitted in British, American, Australian, New Zealand, or Canadian English. Articles should be between 5,000 and 8,000 words, excluding footnotes. Articles are to be sent to the Editor and book reviews to the Book Review Editors.

Editor: Michael A G Haykin, FRHistS
Chair & Professor of Church History
& Director, The Andrew Fuller Center for Baptist Studies
The Southern Baptist Theological Seminary, Louisville, Kentucky
mhaykin@sbts.edu

Associate editors: Baiyu Andrew Song, PhD cand.
The Southern Baptist Theological Seminary
Louisville, Kentucky
& Part-time lecturer, Redeemer University, Ancaster, Ontario
bsong677@students.sbts.edu

Design editor: Dustin W. Benge, PhD
Provost & Professor in Church History
Union School of Theology, Bridgend, Wales

Book review editors: Josiah Michael Claassen, PhD cand.
The Southern Baptist Theological Seminary, Louisville, Kentucky
jclaassen800@students.sbts.edu

C. Anthony Neel, PhD cand.
The Southern Baptist Theological Seminary, Louisville, Kentucky
cneel914@students.sbts.edu

Editorial board
Cindy Aalders, DPhil
Director of the John Richard Allison Library
Assistant Professor of the History of Christianity
Regent College, Vancouver

Ian Hugh Clary, PhD
Assistant Professor of Historical Theology
Colorado Christian University, Lakewood, Colorado

Dustin W. Benge, PhD
Provost & Professor in Church History
Union School of Theology, Bridgend, Wales

Dustin B. Bruce, PhD
Dean & Assistant Professor of Christian Theology and Church History
Boyce College, Louisville, Kentucky

Chris W. Crocker, PhD
Pastor, Markdale Baptist Church, ON
Associate Professor of Church History,
Toronto Baptist Seminary, Ontario

Chris Chun, PhD
Professor of Church History & Director of the *Jonathan Edwards Center*
Gateway Seminary, Ontario, California

Jenny-Lyn de Klerk, PhD
Puritan Project Assistant
Regent College, Vancouver

Jason G. Duesing, PhD
Provost & Professor of Historical Theology
Midwestern Baptist Theological Seminary, Kansas City, Missouri

Nathan A. Finn, PhD
Provost & Dean of the University Faculty
North Greenville University, Tigerville, South Carolina

C. Ryan Griffith, PhD
Independent scholar, Minneapolis, Minnesota

Peter Morden, PhD
Senior Pastor/Team Leader, Cornerstone Baptist Church
Leeds, England
& Distinguished Visiting Scholar
Spurgeon's College, London

Adriaan C. Neele, PhD
Director, Doctoral Program
& Professor of Historical Theology
Puritan Reformed Theological Seminary, Grand Rapids, Michigan
& Research Scholar
Yale University, Jonathan Edwards Center, New Haven, Connecticut

Tom Nettles, PhD
Senior Professor of Historical Theology
The Southern Baptist Theological Seminary, Louisville, Kentucky

Robert Strivens, PhD
Pastor, Bradford on Avon Baptist Church (UK)
& Lecturer in Church History, London Seminary

S. Blair Waddell, PhD
Pastor, Providence Baptist Church, Huntsville, Alabama
& Lecturer in Communications, Church History, & New Testament
The Birmingham Theological Seminary Birmingham, Alabama

Steve Weaver, PhD
Pastor, Farmdale Baptist Church
Frankfort, Kentucky
& Adjunct Professor of Church History
The Southern Baptist Theological Seminary, Louisville, Kentucky

Contents

The Journal of Andrew Fuller Studies
No. 2, February 2021

Editorial Michael A.G. Haykin	9
Articles John Brine and the glory of God's grace Joshua Cook	11
"The dearest of Women is gone": A historical study of grief in the life of John Ryland, Jr. Lon Graham	23
Andrew Fuller and the biblical languages: An exception that proves the rule Chad C. Ashby	45
Texts & documents "The sum and quintessence of all our bliss": a letter of Anne Dutton ed. Michael A.G. Haykin	57
Consolation in spiritual darkness: A letter from Daniel Turner to Benjamin Beddome 1762 ed. Gary Brady	59
An uncatalogued baptism-sermon by Joseph Kinghorn (1766–1832) ed. Baiyu Andrew Song	71
Book Reviews	85

Editorial

Michael A.G. Haykin

Michael A.G. Haykin is Chair and Professor of Church History and Director, The Andrew Fuller Center for Baptist Studies at The Southern Baptist Theological Seminary, Louisville, Kentucky.

In this second issue of *The Journal of Andrew Fuller Studies* we have three essays that provide fresh light on the world of Andrew Fuller. Chad Ashby explores the facility that Fuller, an autodidact, attained with Greek and Hebrew, which were essential to his work as a preacher of the Gospel. Lon Graham examines details of John Ryland's first marriage, a study that I hope will prompt further studies of the familial contexts in which the ministries of Fuller and his friends took place. Finally, Joshua Cook looks at John Brine, a figure usually branded with the epithet of "Hyper-Calvinist," but whose life and thought have never been the object of a full-blown academic study. Joshua Cook's essay is, as it were, a first step in this direction.

This issue also has four documents—by Anne Dutton, Daniel Turner, and two sermons by Joseph Kinghorn—that are a good reminder of the riches that lie in archival deposits as well as in magazines from the eighteenth and nineteenth centuries. And finally there are the book reviews. These are a very important part of a journal like this one, and I would encourage potential reviewers of books about Fuller's global world to contact me at mhaykin@sbts.edu if they can help us in this regard. Enjoy!

The Glory of the Gospel, considered:

IN A

SERMON

PREACHED

At *Kettering* in *Northamptonshire,*

MAY 23, 1762.

✣✣✣✣✣✣✣✣✣✣✣✣✣✣✣✣✣✣✣✣✣✣✣✣
By JOHN BRINE.
✣✣✣✣✣✣✣✣✣✣✣✣✣✣✣✣✣✣✣✣✣✣✣✣

LONDON:
Printed for GEORGE KEITH, in *Gracechurch-street:*
And Sold by JOHN EYNON, Printseller, the
Corner of *Castle-Alley,* by the *Royal-Exchange.*

M DCC LXII.
[Price Six-pence.]

John Brine and the glory of God's grace

Joshua Cook

Joshua Cook is a PhD candidate at The Southern Baptist Theological Seminary, and the Senior Pastor at Our Savior Lutheran Church (LCMS) in Louisville, Kentucky.

Introduction

Joseph Ivimey (1773–1834), the English historian of the eighteenth century, noted that "Mr. [John] Brine was of great weight in the denomination," and that "he was also a very considerable writer."[1] John Brine (1703–1765) was identified by Walter Wilson as a "high" Calvinist, and his reputation in the twentieth and twenty-first centuries has been largely colored by that description, causing him to be viewed in a less-than-favorable light. In the modern era, H. Leon McBeth has linked John Brine to "hyper-Calvinist" John Skepp (d. 1721) because they both served in the pastorate at Cripplegate, and further linked him back to Joseph Hussey (1660–1726) due to Skepp's association as a former Hussey congregant.[2] In concluding his remarks about John Brine, McBeth said, "Like his predecessor, Brine continued the 'noninvitation, nonapplication' style of preaching… Though largely free from the harsh spirit of Skepp, Brine allowed no room for evangelism in his preaching."[3] He also asserted, "Along with Skepp and [John] Gill [1697–1771], Brine did much to fasten hyper-Calvinist views

---

[1] Joseph Ivimey, *History of The English Baptists* (London: B. J. Holdsworth, 1823), 3:367–368.

[2] H. Leon McBeth, *Baptist Heritage* (Nashville, TN: Broadman, 1987), 174–176. This chain of association is not sufficient to prove theological dependence. At best, it may shed light on how Brine could have been exposed to the writings of Hussey, but even this is circumstantial speculation.

[3] McBeth, *Baptist Heritage*, 176.

upon his denomination," and went on to imply that their church, Currier's Hall, suffered decline under Skepp and Brine as a result of this hyper-Calvinism.[4]

This article seeks to begin to examine the theology of John Brine from his own writings in an attempt to understand him in his own words, apart from the opinions transmitted about him from previous generations. In particular, this article seeks to understand why the people of his denomination and his own generation revered him to be a theologian "of great weight."[5]

Brief biography
John Brine was born in 1703 in Kettering to a poor family that could not afford "scarcely any advantages in respect to his education."[6] Brine was baptized in 1718 by Thomas Wallis in the Baptist church in Kettering that was founded by William Wallis (d. 1715) after "having received his first religious impressions from the ministry of his intimate friend Mr. John Gill."[7] Although six years his elder, John Gill became a life-long friend of Brine and the two would work closely together for the rest of their lives. Even before either man entered the public ministry Walter Wilson records that both Gill and Brine worked "for some considerable time" at the "staple manufactory of his native town."[8] During this time, Brine "embraced every opportunity to cultivate his mind, and at an early age had acquired a respectable acquaintance with the learned languages and with other branches of useful knowledge."[9] Brine treasured his copy of *Hutter's Hebrew Bible* which he had received from his father-in-law, John

---

[4] McBeth, *Baptist Heritage*, 176. The statement by Ivimey does not necessarily imply that the reduced numbers at Currier's Hall was the result of Brine's hyper-Calvinism, but McBeth infers the decline to have been caused by the theology. See Ivimey, *History of The English Baptists*, 3:373. McBeth has repeated this claim in his *Sourcebook For Baptist Heritage* (Nashville, TN: Broadman, 1990), 116, when he says: "Brine's theology allowed no room for evangelistic preaching and thus, not surprisingly, his church declined severely."

[5] Ivimey, *History of The English Baptists*, 3:367–368.

[6] Walter Wilson, *History and Antiquities of Dissenting Churches and Meeting Houses* (Repr. Paris, AR: Baptist Standard Bearer, 2003), 2:574.

[7] Ivimey, *History of The English Baptists*, 3:367. George Ella, "John Brine (1703–1765) and His Contemporaries as Seen by Modern Revisionists Part I: Brine's Life." *Biographia Evangelica* (blog), http://evangelica.de/articles/john-brine-1703-1765-and-his-contemporaries-as-seen-by-modern-revisionists-part-i-brines-life/ (accessed August 23, 2019). According to George Ella, the church that Wallis pastored was referred to as the *Little Meeting* after it separated from the principal Reformed congregation of Kettering, the *Great Meeting*, over the issue of baptism. Both John Gill and John Brine belonged to Wallis' congregation.

[8] Wilson, *History and Antiquities*, 2:574.

[9] Ivimey, *History of The English Baptists*, 3:367.

Moore, upon marrying his daughter, Anne.[10] Brine himself was called into the ministry at Kettering and was soon called to lead the church at Coventry. While at Coventry he received funds from the Baptist Fund to purchase books for the furtherance of this education.[11] In 1730 Brine was called to serve in London at the Baptist congregation at Curriers' Hall, Cripplegate, where John Skepp had formerly served. Brine also became a lecturer at Great Eastcheap upon the resignation of John Gill from that lectureship. John Brine was a highly-respected pastor in Baptist circles, and Wilson notes: "The weight that he acquired with his brethren, occasioned his being frequently called upon to preach at the ordination of younger ministers, and to improve the deaths of ministers and private Christians."[12]

After serving more than thirty-five years in London, John Brine died on February 21, 1765.[13] Brine left instructions that he was not to have a funeral sermon preached in his commemoration, which was duly observed, although John Gill offered some concluding comments on his friend's death in a sermon that he preached to his own congregation entitled, *By The Grace of God I Am What I Am*, which were the reported last words of his dear friend.[14] Gill's brief comments demonstrated his admiration for his friend, and his judgment that Brine was an exemplary servant of the Gospel:

> I am debarred from saying so much of him as otherwise I could do, we both being born in the same place, and myself some years older than him, and from his being among the first fruits of my ministry. I might take notice of his natural and acquired abilities, his great understanding, clear light, and sound judgment in the doctrines of the gospel, and the great and deep things of God. Of his zeal, skill, and courage in vindicating important truths, published by him to the world, by which *he being dead, yet speaketh*. In fine, I might observe to you that his walk and conversation in the world was honorable and ornamental to the profession which he made, and suitable to the character he sustained as a minister of Jesus Christ, all which endeared him to his friends. But I am forbid to

---

[10] Wilson, *History and Antiquities*, 2:575; Peter Toon, *Emergence of Hyper-Calvinism in English Nonconformity, 1689–1765* (London: Olive Tree, 1967), 100.

[11] Ivimey, *History of The English Baptists*, 3:367.

[12] Wilson, *History and Antiquities*, 2:576.

[13] Wilson, *History and Antiquities*, 2:576, 579. Wilson actually records this date incorrectly, stating that Brine died on February 24, whereas Ivimey records the date as February 21 in *History of The English Baptists*, 3:371. The error in Wilson's account may be due to editing, as Wilson's own record of Brine's tombstone inscription records February 21 as the correct date a few pages later.

[14] Wilson, *History and Antiquities*, 2:576.

speak any more.[15]

The place of reason and logical refutation in John Brine's writings
Although there has not been much written about John Brine, much of what has been stated about him has been critical, in part because of a view that he allowed reason to play too important a role in his theology. Writing of Brine in 1808, Walter Wilson says:

> More doctrinal than practical, he abounds rather in the discussion of religious subjects according to his own particular apprehensions, than in their application to the conscience … He was generally reputed a high Calvinist; but he went into all the unintelligible depths of the supralapsarian scheme, such as Calvin himself never allowed.[16]

In order to understand John Brine's approach to reason and theology, it is important to understand him in the rationalistic context of the eighteenth century. Raymond Brown notes,

> [Brine] believed that Calvinist of all shades should identify a common enemy in rationalist theology and not dissipate their energies by in-fighting. He urged both parties to recognize 'how numerous they are already, who oppose those important principles, wherein, you are agreed, and that the number of such is increasing every day.'[17]

John Brine regarded Arminianism, Socinianism (or Unitarianism), and Arianism as the greatest threats to the church. Brine believed that it was his responsibility as a minister of God's Word to defend the church against such errors.[18] He took particular offence to anything that would impugn the glory of the grace God, no matter how much it seemed to be in harmony with reason. When preaching at the ordination of John Ryland, Sr. (1723–1792), Brine admonished him to test whether or not a doctrine was true by querying:

> If it exalts the glory of the grace of God, as the sole and entire cause of salvation: if it humbles the creature, and excludes all boasting: if it provides for the honor of the law and justice of God; if it is a solid and sure

---

[15] Wilson, *History and Antiquities*, 2:576–577.

[16] Wilson, *History and Antiquities*, 2:577.

[17] Raymond Brown, *English Baptists of the Eighteenth Century* (London: Baptist Historical Society, 1986), 75.

[18] Toon, *Emergence of Hyper-Calvinism*, 101.

ground of strong consolation to the saints: if it is a doctrine according to Godliness.[19]

Yet, Brine did not despise reason itself, and was more than willing to use reason to make a defense of the truths found in God's Word. Brine instructed Ryland to preach with an understanding that

> There are infallible rules, whereby you may form your judgement of doctrines. No principle can be true, which is not calculated to subserve and secure these important ends; and, therefore, it will be your wisdom to examine all sentiments in divinity by them, and, as you shall find them agreeing, or disagreeing with those rules, embrace or reject them.[20]

By using reason to examine "all sentiments" according to the revealed doctrines of God's Word, Brine believed that a minister would be equipped in the important work of reproving. Continuing to instruct Ryland, Brine recommended four principles for "vindicating the truth":

> 1st. Endeavor clearly to prove one principle, which makes way for and leads on unto other principles, and from which they follow.
> 2ndly. You must show how those Principles, which you design to establish, result from or follow upon that doctrine; whereof evident proof is already given.
> 3rdly. It will be expected of you to answer objections. In doing which you must observe what fallacy is in them, and labor to make that plain, which will be sufficient refutation of them.
> 4thly. Let your proofs of a doctrine be clear testimonies of Scripture. By which I do not mean, that the proposition you intend to prove, must be in so many and in such a form of words found in the Scripture; but that the sense of that proposition is agreeable to the Word of God.[21]

John Brine practiced what he preached. Throughout Brine's preaching and writing a sharply-honed intellect is observed which makes careful arguments against objections to his assertions and crafts conclusions that he believed were flawless. His sermons often include statements that indicate that confidence; for example, he says,

---

[19] John Brine, *Solemn Charge of a Christian Minister Considered: A Sermon Preached at the Ordination of the Reverend Mr. John Ryland, on the 26th of July, 1750* (London: John Ward, 1750), 6.

[20] Brine, *Solemn Charge*, 6–7.

[21] Brine, *Solemn Charge*, 22–23.

Such are the evidences, in favor of this most glorious and precious truth, of our eternal redemption, by the death of the Son of God, that it will never be possible, for the depraved wit of men, to obscure them, by their most sophistical cavils, and objections. We shall certainly be able to triumph over them all, in strictly attending unto, and properly arguing upon, those clear and shining evidences of it.[22]

His confidence came from the fact that his reasoning was founded upon God's revealed truth. While some today may fault Brine for going beyond what Scripture explicitly reveals, Brine demonstrated a confidence in his logical conclusions because he was beginning from God's premises and believed that his conclusions must be true if there were no faults in his logic.[23] Peter Toon observes: "These men [Lewis Wayman (d. 1764), Gill, and Brine] believed that they were not being rationalistic in a human sense but were simply applying 'evangelical reason,' or reason inspired by the Holy Spirit, to the Bible's teaching."[24]

The Sovereignty of God and the Glory of his Grace
If a doctrine must be chosen to describe John Brine's theology that draws it all together and appears to be the "head" of his logical system, it is difficult to decide between such things as his view of election, or the covenants, or Federalism, etc. Perhaps this is due to Brine's careful weaving together of many doctrines to support his arguments. In these arguments, it is difficult to discern one doctrine as more "important" than the other because Brine treats them as complimentary, and therefore equally and mutually necessary. When one steps back and considers Brine's many arguments as a whole, however, a reasonable case can be made that Brine's theology is defending the sovereignty of God with an emphasis on the glory of God's grace.

Much of John Brine's theology is a discussion of the implications of the covenant of grace. What follows is a brief summary of Brine's theological understanding of the covenant of grace and the covenant of works; Adam's and Christ's roles as federal heads of the covenants; and the proper preaching of law and gospel. For Brine, these theological convictions built upon and followed

---

[22] John Brine, *Gospel not absurd: A Sermon Preached April the 13th, 1757* (London: John Ward, 1757), 22.

[23] This author can only speculate on this specific point because an objection to Brine's argument going beyond revelation has not been uncovered as of yet in this author's study of Brine's writings, and therefore the manner in which he would reply is unknown. However, based upon Brine's fourth point under "Reprove" in *Solemn Charge*, as quoted above, it is clear that Brine did not hold to a strict biblicist understanding of reasoning for doctrines only mentioned explicitly in Scripture.

[24] Toon, *Emergence of Hyper-Calvinism*, 147.

from one another. References to the works where these theological points are made will be given in the footnotes.

First, when God created Adam he created him in his image and placed him in Paradise. As the head of humanity God entered into the covenant of works with Adam wherein God promised life to Adam (the federal head of humanity) and his descendants if he would follow God's commands.[25] In this state Adam was righteous and his will, affections, and intellect were all perfect.[26] Because Adam was perfect, he was not obligated to trust in Christ as his Savior from his sins because he had not yet sinned.[27] Therefore, Adam's nature did not include a disposition to trust in Christ because it was unnecessary.[28] God does not give a capacity unless it can be realized.[29]

Then, God knew that Adam would fall. The three persons of the Trinity eternally covenanted with one another to save humanity in such a way that God's grace and glory would be magnified and that the glory of his law and his divine justice would in no way be hindered (an attribute God himself could not have set aside).[30] The Father covenanted with the Son in the covenant of grace that if the Son, as the new federal head of humanity, would take upon himself the consequence of Adam's fall, the Father would impute the righteousness of Christ to all the elect and impute all their unrighteousness to Christ.[31] The Son's

---

[25] Brine, *Solemn Charge*, 14–15; idem, *Defence [sic] of the Doctrine of Eternal Justification, from Some Exceptions made to it By Mr. Bragge, and others* (London: A. Ward, 1732), 41, 63; idem, *Animadversions Upon The Letters on Theron and Aspasio, Addressed to that Ingenious Author* (London: J. Ward, 1758), 7.

[26] John Brine, *Refutation of Arminian Principles, Delivered in a Pamphlet, intitled, [sic] the Modern Question Concerning Repentance and Faith, examined with Candour, &c. in a Letter to a Friend* (London: A. Ward, 1743), 5; idem, *Opposition of Flesh and Spirit in Believers, considered: In A Sermon Preached February the 8th, 1761* (London: George Keith, 1761), 5–15.

[27] Brine, *Refutation of Arminian Principles*, 5, 19.

[28] Brine, *Refutation of Arminian Principles*, 5; idem, *Antidote Against a Spreading Antinomian Principle* (London: John Ward, 1750), 22–23.

[29] Brine, *Refutation of Arminian Principles*, 5–6.

[30] John Brine, *Covenant of Grace Opened: In A Sermon Occasioned by the Death of Mrs. Margaret Busfield, Who Departed this Life, May 13rd, 1734* (London: Aaron Ward, 1734), 25–27; idem, *Job's Epitaph Explained: A Sermon Occasioned by the Death of Mrs. Elizabeth Turner, Who Departed this Life, October 14th, 1755* (London: Aaron Ward, 1755), 21–22; idem, *Solemn Charge*, 6–7; idem, *Antidote Against A Spreading Antinomian Principle*, 42–43; idem, *Animadversions*, 7–8.

[31] John Brine, *The Glory of the Gospel, Considered: In A Sermon Preached At Kettering in Northamptonshire, May 23rd, 1762* (London: George Keith, 1762), 10–15; idem, *Covenant of Grace Opened*, 10–16; idem, *Proper Eternity of the Divine Decrees and of the Mediatorial Office, of Jesus Christ: Asserted and Proved, In a Discourse delivered, in a Monthly Exercise of Prayer with a Sermon, on the 19th of September, 1754* (London: John Ward, 1754), 19–21; idem, *Gospel not absurd*, 18–20; idem, *Solemn Charge*, 3–4; idem, *Defence [sic] of the Doctrine of Eternal Justification*, 41.

willingness to be placed under the law, his active and passive obedience to the law, and his innocent sufferings on humanity's behalf meant that he became the surety of all the elect from eternity (there is no distinction between the Old and New Testament saints).[32] The Holy Spirit covenanted to be the means of the incarnation, to work regeneration in the elect, and to apply what the Father and the Son had done to the elect through his sanctifying work.[33]

Third, by entering into this covenant of grace from eternity God effectively and actually justified all the elect in Christ Jesus as their federal head from eternity (even as all humanity became transgressors of the covenant of works before their existence in the sinful act of their federal head, Adam).[34]

Moreover, all humanity remains condemned under the covenant of works, and all are duty bound to obey the law's demands, even the elect.[35] The perfect obedience that the law demands cannot be rendered by any man, even the elect.[36] Fallen humanity does not have the perfect intellect, will, or affections that the law demands and are thereby at enmity with God.[37] Even God cannot make enmity, love without transgressing his justice.[38] There is nothing in man that can be "rehabilitated" and used toward his own salvation.[39] The spiritual deadness of the old Adam cannot recognize its sinfulness, nor can it trust in Christ.[40] Only God can save his elect by giving them a new heart.[41]

Fifth, although the elect have been justified from eternity, even after their regeneration they remain transgressors of the law and will experience God's temporal wrath as a result, even though God beholds them through Christ as righteous.[42] The Holy Spirit uses the means of God's word to work regeneration

---

[32] Brine, *Covenant of Grace Opened*, 23–24; idem, *Job's Epitaph Explained*, 6, 19; idem, *Proper Eternity of the Divine Decrees*, 26; idem, *Gospel not absurd*, 18–20; idem, *Animadversions*, 9–10.

[33] Brine, *Covenant of Grace Opened*, 25; idem, *Proper Eternity of the Divine Decrees*, 20.

[34] Brine, *Glory of the Gospel, Considered*, 8; idem, *Covenant of Grace Opened*, 22–23; idem, *Gospel not absurd*, 18–20; idem, *Solemn Charge*, 7–8; idem, *Defence [sic] of the Doctrine of Eternal Justification*, 16.

[35] Brine, *Gospel not absurd*, 13–15; idem, *Solemn Charge*, 9–10.

[36] Brine, *Gospel not absurd*, 24–25; idem, *Defence [sic] of the Doctrine of Eternal Justification*, 8–9.

[37] Brine, *Job's Epitaph Explained*, 31.

[38] Brine, *Antidote Against A Spreading Antinomian Principle*, 5–7.

[39] Brine, *Gospel not absurd*, 23, 25; idem, *Antidote Against A Spreading Antinomian Principle*, 5–7; idem, *Defence [sic] of the Doctrine of Eternal Justification*, 14–15; idem, *Opposition of the Flesh and the Spirit*, 16.

[40] Brine, *Solemn Charge*, 15–16.

[41] Brine, *Gospel not absurd*, 9.

[42] Brine, *Covenant of Grace Opened*, 37; idem, *Solemn Charge*, 9–10, 19; idem, *Defence [sic] of the Doctrine of Eternal Justification*, 77–78; idem, *Animadversions*, 27.

and sanctification in the elect. The law is to be preached to convict people (elect and non-elect) of their transgressions against God and his just condemnation of them.[43] Obedience to the law can be rendered out of duty by the non-elect and out of true obedience according to the regenerate nature of the elect.[44] The gospel is to be preached in such a way that the salvation of the elect can in no way be attributed to themselves but only to the gracious work of God, yet the gospel is to be preached even to those who oppose it.[45] The gospel is the source of consolation and hope for the elect and informs them of the saving work of God from eternity on their behalf and enumerates the blessings of their inheritance.[46] Natural man cannot and does not approve of the gospel, hence, approving of the gospel is evidence of illumination from God.[47]

Sixth and final, "offering" God's grace is inappropriate because it implies that man has a natural disposition to trust Christ and that God rewards faith with the justification of the sinner.[48] By making faith into a duty of the Gospel, the law of God is dishonored because Christ's death on the cross is said to abrogate the old law and put in its place the new law of faith.[49] Instead of perfection, this new law would only require that one respond to the offer of God's grace in Christ Jesus. This is to make faith into a work of man.[50] Instead, it must be recognized that men are not justified by faith.[51] The elect have been justified eternally by God's just decree in the covenant of grace whereby he has agreed to give his elect all the blessings in Christ Jesus by his grace, including justification and faith.[52] When Scripture speaks of the being justified by faith it is speaking

---

[43] Brine, *Gospel not absurd*, 23.

[44] Brine, *Glory of the Gospel, Considered*, 26; idem, *The Solemn Charge*, 31–32; idem, *A Refutation of Arminian Principles*, 11–12.

[45] Brine, *Gospel not absurd*, 24–25, 28-30; idem, *Refutation of Arminian Principles*, 20–21, 44–45.

[46] Brine, *Glory of the Gospel, Considered*, 5; idem, *Covenant of Grace Opened*, 37–38.

[47] Brine, *Glory of the Gospel, Considered*, 4; idem, *Proper Eternity of the Divine Decrees*, 35–37; idem, *Gospel not absurd*, 2.

[48] Brine, *Antidote Against A Spreading Antinomian Principle*, 9–10, 18; idem, *Refutation of Arminian Principles*, 10–11, 21–22.

[49] Brine, *Antidote Against A Spreading Antinomian Principle*, 2–3, 9; idem, *Animadversions*, 23–24.

[50] Brine, *Antidote Against A Spreading Antinomian Principle*, 4, 18 idem, *Defence [sic] of the Doctrine of Eternal Justification*, 14; idem, *Refutation of Arminian Principles*, 36.

[51] Brine, *Antidote Against A Spreading Antinomian Principle*, 15; idem, *Defense of the Doctrine of Eternal Justification*, 6–7, 9.

[52] Brine, *Covenant of Grace Opened*, 28–29; idem, *Antidote Against A Spreading Antinomian Principle*, 36–37; idem, *Defence [sic] of the Doctrine of Eternal Justification*, 16.

about the recognition of the Christian of his eternal justification in Christ—it is the subjective perception of the objective eternal reality.[53]

From this summary, it can be observed that Brine places great moment upon the consequences of the covenant of grace. For Brine, the glory of God's grace is magnificent in splendor, and the covenant of grace is perfectly designed to highlight the Trinity's benevolence. The salvation of the elect springs from the willing choice that the Son makes to humble and submit himself to the covenant of works and to suffer under the law's curse as redeemer and federal head for those whom the Father has given him. The Father delights in the Son's willing acceptance of the covenant of grace which he proposed to the Son that results in the Father's assurance that he will impute the righteousness of the Son to the elect and their unrighteousness to the Son, accepting him as their surety and atoning sacrifice. The Holy Spirit also participates and delights in this covenant from eternity and promises his active role in applying the benefits of this glorious plan of grace to the elect. In this way, the entire Trinity participates in this eternal plan of grace, designed to accomplish the salvation of the elect and to magnify the glory of God's grace without diminishing in any way his justice or the glory of the law.

Far from being an Antinomian, Brine considers his system of theology to be the only one that both preserves the glory of the law and its enduring permanence, and absolutely limits any grounds for boasting that man had any role in effecting his own salvation. Preaching both the law and gospel is absolutely necessary, although only God's elect will be "internally" keepers of the law or recognizers of themselves as the recipients of God's grace.

Conclusion

Brine's critics have faulted his hyper-Calvinism and supralapsarianism as causing him to fall into a determinism that eradicated man's responsibility and led to his support of the "no offer of grace" position. This may be a valid critique. However, as is the case with the partial rethinking of John Gill, perhaps Brine's reputation should also be re-evaluated after further study has been made of his works, rather than merely repeating the sentiments of the past.[54] John Brine's astute intellect was able to discern the slightest hint of human effort that would ultimately rob God of his glory, and he defended the Particular Baptists from

---

[53] Brine, *Defence [sic] of the Doctrine of Eternal Justification*, 11–12, 38–39, 68–69.

[54] For arguments for and against a new understanding of Gill see Tom Nettles, *By His Grace and for His Glory: A Historical, Theological, and Practical Study of the Doctrines of Grace in Baptist Life* (Grand Rapids: Baker Book House, 1986), 106–107; R.W. Oliver, "John Gill (1697–1771)," in *The British Particular Baptists, 1638–1910*, ed. Michael A.G. Haykin (Springfield, MO: Particular Baptist Press, 1998), 1:162; Peter Naylor, *Calvinism, Communion, and the Baptists: A Study of English Calvinistic Baptists from the Late 1600s to the Early 1800s*, Studies in Baptist History and Thought, 7 (Carlisle, Cumbria: Paternoster, 2003), 164–182.

the encroaching rationalistic philosophies and doctrines that led other denominations away from the truth entirely. Brine's hyper-Calvinism is distasteful to most people in the twenty-first century, but in the eighteenth century it was part of the air that Brine and other theologians breathed. Brine was a formidable theologian that pressed for a theology that remained logically consistent with itself. In this way, he believed that the sovereignty of God and the glory of his grace would be honored, and that God's people would be preserved. Perhaps the Particular Baptists of John Brine's day considered him to be a theologian of "great weight" because they appreciated that he was zealous to reserve for God alone the full glory of his grace in the face of a rationalism that gave too great a weight to man's abilities.

"The dearest of Women is gone": A historical study of grief in the life of John Ryland, Jr.[1]

Lon Graham

Lon Graham (PhD, Vrije Universiteit Amsterdam) is the pastor of The Woods Baptist Church in Tyler, Texas.

Introduction

In the archive of Bristol Baptist College, there are two volumes of 165 hand-written poems by John Ryland, Jr. (1753–1825) composed between 1779 and 1821. While Ryland was a published poet, his poetry never reached the audience or critical acclaim of his fellow Bristolian, Samuel Taylor Coleridge. Whatever he lacked in renown, Ryland made up for in consistency: from an early age, Ryland was busy at his poems. He published his first book of poetry at age thirteen, and his last published piece of poetry was written during his final illness in 1825.[2]

Ryland's early poetry is of a distinctly theological bent.[3] This is evidenced

---

[1] An earlier version of this article was first published in *Journal of European Baptist Studies*, 19, no.2 (2019): 66–83. Used with permission.

[2] John Ryland, *The Plagues of Egypt, by a School-boy Thirteen Years of Age* (London, 1766); John Ryland, "Lines Written by the Late Dr. Ryland during His Last Illness," *Baptist Magazine* 17 (1825): 308.

[3] He says of his early poetry, "Since that time [his conversion in 1767], my poems have been chiefly on religious subjects, some of which having been seen by several Christian friends, who have signified their approbation of them, and their desire to have a few of them published, which they hoped might be neither disagreeable nor useless to many of the Lord's people, I was persuaded to consent" (John Ryland, *Serious Essays on the Truths of the Glorious Gospel, and the Various Branches of Vital Experience. For the Use of True Christians* [London: J.W. Pasham, 1771], viii).

by Ryland's early book of poetry entitled *Serious Essays on the Truths of the Glorious Gospel*, which is complete with Scripture proofs after many of the stanzas.[4] While he ceased publishing books of poetry in 1773, he continued to compose poems along the same theologically-motivated lines as before.[5] However, in 1787, the tenor of Ryland's poetry changes, and it becomes more personal. The reason for this is not difficult to discern: Ryland lost his wife, Elizabeth (Betsy), just forty-five days after she gave birth to their first child, a son named John Tyler Ryland. Ryland's reaction to her death has not been examined in depth in any of the recent research into his life and thought. This is likely because of how little it seemed to disturb his public ministry: Betsy died on 23 January 1787, and he was back in the pulpit for the funeral of a child on 2 February.[6] Thereafter, he resumed his ordinary duties as pastor at College Lane, Northampton.

In the light of this, it would be easy, and perhaps reasonable, to assume that Ryland continued his life largely undisturbed after Betsy's death. However, his private writings reveal a deep and lasting pain. In a letter to Jonathan Edwards Jr, Ryland shows the grief he was enduring. After giving an account of their relationship[7] as well as Betsy's last weeks, Ryland says, "Do pray for me! I can pray but seldom with a degree of proper feeling."[8] Ryland also divulged his heart to his frequent counsellors John Newton and Robert Hall, Sr.[9]

It is in the two volumes of poetry, however, that one finds a lengthy, unguarded look into the broken spirit of a man grieving the loss of his wife. It is worth examining because it provides a deeper, fuller picture of who Ryland was as a husband and man. He appears in the poems less as a churchman, pastor, and denominational leader and more as ordinary, struggling man whose theology served both to wound and soothe his soul.

---

[4] Ryland, *Serious Essays*, passim.

[5] John Ryland, *The Faithfulness of God in His Word Evinced* (London: J.W. Pasham, 1773).

[6] John Ryland, "Text Book," 2 February 1787 (Northamptonshire Record Office, Northmapton). Ryland marked the occasion of Betsy's death with a black bar drawn on the date.

[7] Speaking of their married life together, he says, "I lived wth her 7 years. They were 7 years of sore trials in some respects, from another quarter, but she was a blessed comfort to me under them. Few young women ever equall'd her in prudence & every amiable disposition. She had a great degree of domestic œconomy, join'd with much benevolence to the poor" (John Ryland, Jr., Letter to Jonathan Edwards, Jr., 29 June 1787 [Beinecke Rare Book and Manuscript Library, Yale University]). Ryland's description of their relationship to Edwards, Jr., is very much in keeping with what is found in the poems.

[8] Ryland, Letter to Jonathan Edwards, Jr., 29 June 1787.

[9] The letters to Newton and Hall have been lost, but letters from them yet remain and demonstrate that Ryland was open with them about his grief. A letter from Hall is held in the Bristol Baptist College Archives, and the letters from Newton were published in Grant Gordon, ed., *Wise Counsel: John Newton's Letters to John Ryland Jr.* (Edinburgh: Banner of Truth Trust, 2009).

John Ryland and Elizabeth Tyler
Ryland had longed to marry. He says in his "Autograph Reminiscences" that he first began to think of marrying in 1775.[10] As he did not marry Betsy until 1780, that meant five years of waiting. Ryland mentions two young ladies with whom he attempted a courtship, both of which came to naught. These disappointments were apparently quite sore for Ryland at the time. He wrote to Newton about his struggles, and Newton responded with compassionate yet firm counsel. As Ryland was seemingly growing impatient with the process of finding a wife, Newton advises him, saying, "Worldly people expect their schemes to run upon all-fours."[11] He encourages Ryland to trust God to provide for him at the right time: "if he sees the marriage state best for you, he has the proper person already in his eye; and though she were in Peru or Nova-Zembla, he knows how to bring you together. In the mean time, go thou and preach the Gospel."[12] Ryland obeyed the counsel of his mentor and continued his ministry, but his desire to marry did not abate.

So it was in December 1776, Ryland began to court Elizabeth Tyler.[13] She was born on 1 December 1758 to Robert and Elizabeth Tyler of Banbury.[14] Her parents probably died before she came of age, as Newton mentions her being

---

[10] John Ryland, Jr., "Autograph Reminiscences" (Bristol Baptist College Archives, Bristol Baptist College, Bristol), 53.

[11] John Newton, Letter to John Ryland, Jr., 6 July 1776, in Gordon, *Wise Counsel*, 92.

[12] Newton, Letter to John Ryland, Jr., 6 July 1776, in Gordon, *Wise Counsel*, 92. "Nova-Zembla" is most likely Novaya Zemlya, a large and sparsely inhabited island north of Russia that divides the Barents and Kara seas. In the same letter, Newton tells Ryland, "You were sent into the world for a nobler end than to be pinned to a girl's apron-string" (Newton, Letter to John Ryland, Jr., 6 July 1776, in Gordon, *Wise Counsel*, 92). In a later letter, he tries to help Ryland see the positive side of a recent relationship disappointment: "Indeed the one circumstance you mention make me more ready to call it an escape than a disappointment" (John Newton, Letter to John Ryland, Jr., 20 December 1776, in Gordon, *Wise Counsel*, 99). These are all indicative of Newton's letters to Ryland during this time.

[13] The timing of the beginning of the courtship is revealed by Ryland in a note on a hymn he composed 31 December 1776. Ryland writes, "This was made at Bradwin, when I first went over to see Miss Betsy Tyler, whom I married 3 y^{rs}. afterward, & who was Mother to John Tyler Ryland" (John Ryland, *A Selection of Hymns Composed by J Ryland Jnr. Between 1773 and 1778* [Bristol Baptist College Archives, Bristol Baptist College, Bristol], 83). A letter from Newton to Ryland on 7 February 1777 about a new prospective wife aligns with this date.

[14] Anon., *England and Wales, Non-Conformist and Non-Parochial Registers, 1567–1970* (National Archives of the United Kingdom), 80. Her birth record is lost, but her birthdate can be extrapolated from data within the two books of poems. She died on 23 January 1787, and Ryland says that she was aged twenty-eight at the time of her death (John Ryland, *Poems by John Ryland Junr, Vol. 2 [1783–1795]* [Bristol Baptist College Archives, Bristol Baptist College, Bristol], 67). Elsewhere, Ryland writes two poems on Betsy's birthday, which he notes was 1 December. If she was twenty-eight at her death on 23 January 1787, and her birthday was 1 December, then her birth date must be 1 December 1758.

under guardians while at school.[15] While at school, she became a member of College Lane Baptist Church, where Ryland was the co-pastor along with his father.[16] It was in this context that they likely would have first met, though their courting began after she had moved away to Bradwin.[17] The courtship process took three years, and John Ryland, Jr. and Elizabeth Tyler were finally married on 12 January 1780.[18]

On 9 December 1786, Betsy gave birth to John Tyler Ryland. Ryland's joy at the birth of his first son compelled him to take up his pen and write a poem to his son:

My dear little boy
Shall I sit down & try
To make you some verses to learn
That I may please you
And as it is due
Teach you to please me in return.[19]

A pastor's struggle at the death of an affectionate wife
The boy was healthy, but Betsy's health was precarious. Ryland describes her last weeks to Edwards, Jr. After a "painful lingering labor," Betsy was "seized with most violent convulsions."[20] Those around her observed "many tokens of a consumptive nature" in Betsy, and she seems to have slowly declined until she finally passed. Ryland describes her death: "She died very sweetly! I never saw anybody die beside. I had hold of her hand all the while. God took away all her

---

[15] John Newton, Letter to John Ryland, Jr., 7 February 1777, in Gordon, *Wise Counsel*, 103.

[16] Betsy joined the church at College Lane on 8 April 1774 (Anon., "College Lane Baptist Church: Church Book, 1737–1781" [Northamptonshire Record Office, Northampton], 185). She was, at the time, a student at Mrs. Trinder's school for girls (Ryland, Letter to Jonathan Edwards, Jr., 29 June 1787). For more information on Martha Trinder and her school, see Karen E. Smith, "'Female Education' among Baptists in the Eighteenth Century: Martha (Smith) Trinder (1736–1790) and Henrietta Neale (1752–1802)," *Baptist Quarterly* 48, no.4 (2017): 172–176.

[17] See footnote 13. Bradwin is now known as Bradden.

[18] Anon., *Northamptonshire, England, Church of England Marriages, 1754–1912* (Northamptonshire Record Office, Northampton), 8. Cf. Ryland, "Text Book," 12 January 1780.

[19] Ryland, *Poems*, 2:49. His happiness may also be seen in the birth register entry for John Tyler. It is written in Ryland's handwriting, and it takes up noticeably more space than the others on the same page. He includes more information about the family and signs it with a flourish not seen in his other signatures on the page. In a sad coincidence, the facing page, the death registry, contains the entry for Betsy (Anon., *England and Wales, Non-Conformist and Non-Parochial Registers, 1567–1970* [National Archives of the United Kingdom], 80).

[20] Ryland, Letter to Jonathan Edwards, Jr., 29 June 1787.

fears. Tho she was of a very nervous, timid constitution."[21]

Ryland's first poem after Betsy's death begins with an introduction, stating that it is meant as the "prayr of a poor solitary Father for his poor little orphan Boy, design'd at the same time as a memorial of the dearest of all the human race, my precious affectionate Wife, who joined the spirits of the just made perfect Jan. 23. 1787."[22] The language of the poem is that of loss and sorrow mixed with hope and reassurance. Ryland writes of his infant son:

This poor little motherless boy
That lies in my bosom asleep,
From all that w^d. hurt or destroy
I pray the Redeemer to keep.[23]

Of Betsy, Ryland is both despondent and hopeful:

The dearest of Women is gone
Who bore him with sorrow & pain;
I'm left to feel trouble alone;
She never shall sorrow again.
She's gone, but her infant remains;
Sweet pledge of connection so sweet!
Her God her poor husband sustains,
Nor will he her infant forget.[24]

He writes about Betsy's prayers for her new son while she yet lived and how she "gave up her babe to her God."[25] He pictures her in her dying as resigned to the will of God: lying in the arms of her Lord, filled with peace and serenity, silently sinking into rest. Around her deathbed, her loved ones, Ryland in particular, hid their emotions and kept her from seeing their struggles:

Our passions we strove to withhold;
But often by stealth drop'd a tear.[26]

---

[21] Ryland, Letter to Jonathan Edwards, Jr., 29 June 1787.

[22] Ryland, *Poems*, 2:51.

[23] Ryland, *Poems*, 2:51.

[24] Ryland, *Poems*, 2:51.

[25] Ryland, *Poems*, 2:52.

[26] Ryland, *Poems*, 2:53.

In death she is largely idealized, portrayed as free from all the troubles that this world affords: she feels no anxiety and her soul "is all rapture on high."[27] It is interesting to note that the hope found in this early poem is hope for Betsy, not necessarily for Ryland himself. He speaks of "her joy" and "her bliss."[28] For himself, Ryland seems to see darkness with only a little light ahead. He writes:

> O how cou'd I possibly part
> So long & so tenderly ty'd?
> Ten years to the choice of my heart,
> Full sev'n to my loveliest bride![29]

Herein is seen the theological struggle in the poems. Ryland's theology was thoroughly Calvinistic in terms of how he understood the sovereignty of God. At his ordination, he produced a confession of his faith in which he states that he believes that God not only has "Foreknowledge from Eternity of all Events," but that nothing can "alter the most perfect and determinate plan laid down in his decrees who worketh all Things according to the Counsel of his own Will."[30] There is nothing that is exempt from these decrees, and, according to Ryland, "nothing was left out of his original Purpose."[31]

Ryland did not drop his understanding of sovereignty when Betsy passed away. He could speak of death being "at her Savior's command," and that he could not withstand the pleasure of the Lord to call her.[32] However, he dared not say that he felt no pain at the blow. It was a lasting wound, and it was inflicted by the Lord whom he loved. This struggle between owning his pain and knowing it came from the Lord would continue for years, and it is seen most acutely in Ryland's lack of personal engagement with the doctrines he held and preached. That is, for some time after Betsy's death, in his poetry if not his preaching, when Ryland speaks of theological truth, it is generally depersonalized. In this first poem, Ryland's only "engagement" with God is a prayer in the last

---

[27] Ryland, *Poems*, 2:52.

[28] Ryland, *Poems*, 2:53, 54.

[29] Ryland, *Poems*, 2:54.

[30] John Ryland, Jr., "A Confession of Faith" (Bristol Baptist College Archives, Bristol Baptist College, Bristol), 7.

[31] Ryland, "Confession of Faith," 7. This was his settled theological position. Many years later, he would write something similar, saying that God, "'who worketh all things after the counsel of his own will,' cannot be defeated in the execution of his gracious purposes, or disappointed of his desired end" (*The Certain Increase of the Kingdom and Glory of Jesus* [London: Button, 1794], 22).

[32] Ryland, *Poems*, 2:54.

stanza:

> Now Lord be my God & my Guide,
> My friend & companion alone!
> And for my dear Infant provide,
> And seal his young heart for thy own.[33]

A couple of weeks after that poem was penned, John Tyler fell ill. He was not given much hope of recovery, and Ryland once again took up his pen. Again, his theological struggle comes to the fore, as he begins the poem with a question for God:

> Dear dying pledge of my own Betsy's Love,
> Part of myself, as part of her more dear;
> Will Heav'ns great Lord all earthly Joy remove?
> And must his Wisdom leave me nothing here?
> He takes away & who can then withhold?
> Who shall presume to ask him 'What dost thou?'
> Almighty pow'r can never be control'd;
> To perfect rectitude all ought to bow.[34]

He believes that God can heal his son if he will, writing that "one kind volition wou'd O Lord suffice."[35] However, he will not deny the sting of hearing his son's cries, hide his parental anguish, or pretend that he is at ease with the prospect of losing his son so soon after the death of his wife. He openly prays for his son's recovery, but he also soothes his own worries with the hope his son would have of heaven. Ryland's understanding of the after-life of infants dying in infancy is somewhat difficult to discern,[36] but he holds out hope that his

---

[33] Ryland, *Poems*, 2:54.

[34] Ryland, *Poems*, 2:55.

[35] Ryland, *Poems*, 2:55.

[36] The correspondence with Newton includes discussion regarding the subject, with Newton taking the position that infants dying in infancy are received into heaven by the blood of Christ (John Newton, Letter to John Ryland, Jr., 14 May 1799, in Gordon, *Wise Counsel*, 353). At times, Ryland would seem to disagree with Newton, or at least not possess Newton's surety, as he writes in one poem, dated December 1795:

> If ere he taste of earthly Woe
> Or actually can sin,
> Thou shou'dst eternal Life bestow,
> And bid his heavn begin (Ryland, *Poems*, 2:122).

infant son, were he to die, would be with God in heaven. He even offers a prayer that somehow Betsy might instruct John Tyler before his death:

> Perhaps that dear maternal spirit may
> Receive commission to instruct her son;
> Unknown ideas to his mind convey
> By modes to mortals here entomb'd unknown.[37]

A hopeful heavenward gaze

The prospect of his son's death gave Ryland cause to look to his own death, when, he says, he will be reunited with Betsy:

> Which ever first shall his dear Mother meet
> Or he, or I, Oh bring us there at last
> Where each our crowns before the Saviors feet
> In holy extacy shall gladly cast.
> Mother & Father & their only Son
> In the sweet heavnly contest shall agree

An earlier poem, written in March 1787, when he thought that John Tyler might die, is more positive about the destiny of infants:

Speak but the word & my dear babe fhall live;
Pain & disease fhall both thy will obey;
Or to thyself his spirit Lord receive,
To dwell with thee in everlasting day (Ryland, *Poems*, 2:55).

Later, Ryland seems to fully adopt Newton's position, as, in August 1813, he writes to John Tyler to console him on the loss of his daughter, Sophia Elizabeth Ryland, who lived but one day:

Better for your Babe to go,
Where all his Glory see,
Than, in realms of sin & woe,
A pilgrim long to be.

One short day her journey ends,
One day she has to moan,
Then her blood-bought soul ascends,
To stand before the throne.

(*Poems by John Ryland Junr, Vol. 1 (1778–1821)* [Bristol Baptist College Archives, Bristol Baptist College, Bristol], 10–11).

[37] Ryland, *Poems*, 2:56. This is definitely an unusual request by Ryland, as it would require God giving Betsy renewed access to earthly life to communicate with the infant John Tyler Ryland. This is perhaps some evidence of the depth of Ryland's pain at this point.

Disputing then this single point alone
Which was the deepest Lord in debt to Thee.[38]

In Ryland's earlier poetry, he focuses on the service he can offer Christ in this life. For example, in a hymn he wrote to Betsy during their courtship, Ryland writes:

Lord & is this blessing ours?
Thee we'd praise with all our powrs.
We are thine, thou are our choice,
All our souls in thee rejoice.[39]

His spirituality in the earlier hymn is a present, earthly spirituality. The spirituality of the poem is much more future- and heaven-oriented. Ryland's gaze is turned away from this world and its vale of sorrows and tears and to heaven.

The next poem Ryland records in this volume is a musing on Psalm 88:18, which reads, "You have caused my beloved and my friend to shun me; my companions have become darkness." In light of this psalm, Ryland owns that it is the Lord who has taken Betsy from him:

Lover & friend, O Lord, has thou
Put far away from me;
My best acquaintance here below
I never more shall see.[40]

Ryland speaks of God's ability to meet every need of his people: "ev'ry loss thou canst supply."[41] Ryland believes this to be true, at least, theoretically. His own experience, however, is that his losses have not been supplied. They are, rather, laid heavy upon him:

Bereav'd & desolate I am,
And heavily opprest.[42]

---

[38] Ryland, *Poems*, 2:58.

[39] John Ryland, *A Selection of Hymns Composed by J Ryland Jnr. Between 1773 and 1778* (Bristol Baptist College Archives, Bristol Baptist College, Bristol), 87.

[40] Ryland, *Poems*, 2:59.

[41] Ryland, *Poems*, 2:59.

[42] Ryland, *Poems*, 2:59.

He goes on to say that he still trusts in "thy Name," and he looks to the Lord for refuge and rest, but it is worthwhile to note that these are hopeful attainments for Ryland rather than present possessions. His theology tells him that God can assuage every grief and meet every need, but his experience is telling him that that has not happened for him. All he is left with is this poetic prayer, asking God to conduct him to the "fountain head," in which "all are fill'd above." He identifies this fountain head as the place where those around us "never for a moment dread the ebbing of thy Love."[43] This would indicate that Ryland was not at that time free of such dread. The loss of Betsy, understood in light of God's sovereign rule over all events, was not necessarily a loss of faith for Ryland; it was, however, a crisis of confidence in his own experience of God's love.

The next poem is to John Tyler on 27 November 1787, twelve days before his birthday. Apparently, Betsy began her labor on this day twelve months prior.[44] The poem itself is chiefly a remembrance of Betsy for John. He describes her face as place "where lilies mix'd with roses grew," and he points out that Betsy had a strawberry birthmark beneath her eye.[45] Again, Betsy is idealized as a perfect specimen of a saint. Her mind was so beautiful that he lacks the poetic ability to describe it. Every grace was combined in her, "the lovely Saint."[46] Ryland's purpose in the poems seems to be to assure John Tyler of his mother's character and love. While she and John Tyler were both alive, "her spirit staid and hover'd o'er her Son," praying for both him and his father.[47] He points John Tyler to the hope of resurrection, in which "Mamma shall rise again ... when death itself is slain," for it is in that place that they will all be together again.[48]

Ryland next addresses Betsy's death in a poem on what would have been her twenty-ninth birthday. Ryland favors the juxtaposition between himself and Betsy, which is seen in other poems but especially clear in this one. He speaks of his loneliness and portrays himself as a "weary pilgrim" creeping through a thorny maze, while Betsy enjoys heavenly bliss:

<u>She needs not</u> creatures to augment her bliss,

[43] Ryland, *Poems*, 2:59.

[44] Ryland makes reference to this:

How soon are XII months fled,
Since your dear Mother's pangs came on?
(Ryland, *Poems*, 2:60).

[45] Whether it was shaped or colored like a strawberry is unknown.

[46] Ryland, *Poems*, 2:60.

[47] Ryland, *Poems*, 2:60.

[48] Ryland, *Poems*, 2:61.

From God himself her living comforts flow:
And evil cannot enter where she is,
Nor terror nor temptation reach her now.[49]

He looks again to the return of Christ and the resurrection of the just. However, his hope in this case is focused on Betsy's rise:

Her slumbering clay that joyful trump shall hear,
And in immortal youth & beauty rise;
The likeness of her blessed Savior wear,
And dwell forever with him in the skies.[50]

Heaven is portrayed in this poem less as the place of God's dwelling and more as the house of departed loved ones. Ryland speaks more of friends and people whom he admired being in heaven with Betsy than he does anything else. These include friends such as David Evans of Thorn, Hannah Payen Law, and Mary Vaughan, as well as theologians and ministers which Ryland admired, such as James Hervey, Joseph Bellamy, Jonathan Edwards, David Brainerd, John Owen, Stephen Charnock, Joseph Alleine, and John Maclaurin.[51] Ryland's attention in this poem is focused almost exclusively on the people with whom he expects to have communion in heaven, whether he knew them personally or through their writings. Evans is "clad in light divine," Law and Vaughan shine with Betsy, Bellamy (who "plac'd 'true Religion' in a clearer Light") is also portrayed as shining bright, and Alleine glows with "celestial Fire."[52]

Ryland's expectation for himself is largely limited to meeting Betsy and being introduced by her to people whom he has admired.[53] Indeed, it is the "sweet hope" of being with them that sustains what he calls his "burden'd mind."[54] As he closes the poem, Ryland's mind wanders back to his beloved Betsy:

My soul's best half is now already there,
  And there, her God, my All, for ever reigns.[55]

---

[49] Ryland, *Poems*, 2:62.

[50] Ryland, *Poems*, 2:63.

[51] Ryland, *Poems*, 2:64–66.

[52] Ryland, *Poems*, 2:64–65.

[53] He does mention anticipating having his "last Abode" with Christ, but this is limited to one line amidst the many stanzas related to seeing the others (Ryland, *Poems*, 2:66).

[54] Ryland, *Poems*, 2:66.

[55] Ryland, *Poems*, 2:62–66.

Anticipating heaven as a place of reunion with departed loved ones is, in many ways, an extension of Ryland's understanding of the church catholic. Ryland's catholicity was well-known in his day, and it extended beyond the bounds of earthly life.[56] Ryland believed in the church militant and the church triumphant, and the death of a saint meant the dismissal from the former into the latter.[57] He writes of the state of believers after death, "The S^{ts}. are X^{ts}. Friends as well as ours, & we must allow him to have his blessed Will (Joh. xvii. 24.) to have his friends about him, as well as we have had them so long; and it may be, before X^t. has had them so long with him, as some of us have had them here below, we shall be with them again, and Christ, and they, and we shall be all together! O what a happy Meeting! They & we freed of all natural & sinful Infirmities. There θe Communion of S^{ts}. is in perfection, & this blessed Society shall never break up or separate. No parting Salutation there. The word Farewell is no part of the heavenly Language."[58]

The idea of reunion with Betsy, coupled with his understanding of heaven as a reunion of believing friends, returns in the next poem in which he references Betsy, which was written on their wedding anniversary.[59] Ryland begins in a

[56] In the funeral sermon for Ryland, Robert Hall, Jr. comments on his departed friend's broad friendships, saying, "Though a Calvinist, in the strictest sense of the word, and attached to its peculiarities in a higher degree than most of the advocates of that system, he extended his affection to all who bore the image of Christ, and was ingenious in discovering reasons for thinking well of many who widely dissented from his religious views. No man was more remarkable for combining a zealous attachment to his own principles with the utmost liberality of mind towards those who differed from him; an abhorrence of error, with the kindest feelings towards the erroneous. He detested the spirit of monopoly in religion, and opposed every tendency to circumscribe it by the limits of party" (Hall, "A Sermon," 398).

[57] Preaching the funeral for a Mrs. A. Tozer in 1820, Ryland begins, "You are generally aware that God has lately removed from the Ch. militant to the Ch. triumph^t. a very excell^t. Person, who has had Communion wth. this X^n Society ab^t. 25 yrs" ("Sermon Notes: 2 Samuel 23:5," *Original Manuscript Sermons: Old Testament, Vol. I* [Bristol Baptist College Archives, Bristol Baptist College, Bristol]).

[58] Ryland, "Sermon Notes: 2 Samuel 23:5." "S^{ts}" is Ryland's short for "saints" and "X^{ts}" stands for "Christ's." "θe" is short for "the."

[59] Between this poem and the last Ryland inserts a draft of the epitaph he had written for Betsy, whom he calls "the dearest of all Women" (Ryland, *Poems*, 2:67). It begins: "ELIZABETH RYLAND, the eldest Daughter of Rob. & Eliz. Tyler, & for seven years the affectionate & beloved Wife of John Ryland jun^r. enter into the Joy of her Lord Jan. 23. 1787. Aged 28. Years" (Ryland, *Poems*, 2:67). Ryland includes several drafts and additions to the epitaph, with the following seemingly final version:

The Tomb a while detains her Clay
But Vict'ry crown'd her dying Day
Death's pointless Dart her Savior broke
She smil'd to feel its harmless stroke
Which had no power to destroy
Her blood-bought soul, her heavn-born joy

solemn tone:

> Once happy day! but ah how gloomy now,
> When recollection fills my breast wth. Woe![60]

The poem fits well with the previous poems directed to or about Betsy. He speaks repeatedly of her present joy and her advantage in death.[61] He also recognizes the role that God played in her death:

> Scarse was it past, when soon a voice divine
> Said "come up hither" & my Love obey'd:[62]

What makes this particular poem unique is Ryland's emphasis on his present relationship to Betsy and its future prospect.[63] While the hope of their reunion is found elsewhere, in poems both before and after this, the way in which Ryland expresses himself is unusual. He speaks of the "string wth. wch. our hearts were closely ty'd" being presently broken by her death, but he goes on to write of another that "Death cou'd not divide," which is now "stretch'd to heav'n," and which "must & will remain."[64] This unbroken string that binds them together is "sacred Love far stronger than before" that "bind her to Jesus, & to all his friends." At first glance, it would seem as though Ryland is merely resting here

---

(Ryland, *Poems*, 2:67).

[60] Ryland, *Poems*, 2:69.

[61] She is "breath divine" and "immortal—no, she cou'd not die" (Ryland, *Poems*, 2:70).

[62] Ryland, *Poems*, 2:69.

[63] This poem is also noteworthy for containing one of the few references to words that Betsy herself spoke. It is not known when she spoke these words, but it seems from the context that it was during her last illness:

> We 'are the Babies'—true, my Betsy, true—
> Those words mysterious now I understand;
> We shall not reach full age till we, with you,
> Are safe translated to Immanuel's Land
> (Ryland, *Poems*, 2:72).

On the facing page, Ryland inserts a poetic note meant to elaborate on the second line:

> Was it thy spirit from the realms of joy
> That to explain thy dying language came?
> Or did thy God more common means employ
> To form so pleasant & so true a dream?

[64] He says that is it "broke, & bleeds—I feel it throb with pain" (Ryland, *Poems*, 2:70).

on the connection that all saints have in Christ, but he goes on to speak of the peculiar reunion and joy that he and Betsy would share.[65] He understands their bond to be unique and unbroken by death. She is his "Soul's best friend," with whom no other earthly friendship could compare, of whom he could say that not even his own body was even half as dear.[66] He writes:

> But <u>we</u> if met in heav'n, must sure enjoy
> A special pleasure in other's bliss;
> That World will sinful Selfishness destroy,
> But not obliterate th' Events of this.[67]

While in that place "from sensual passions are the saints refin'd," and while he would have stipulated in his wedding vows that his bond to Betsy was to be broken at death, Ryland believes, nevertheless, that his bond with Betsy continued after her death and would be resumed, though in a different form, at his.[68] His thinking seems to run thus: if death does not break the bonds of friendship, then surely it does not destroy the much deeper bond that he and Betsy shared.

The darkness begins to lift
The first poem that Ryland wrote after Betsy's death that did not have to do with either Betsy or John was not written until over a year after her death. On 26 February 1788, Ryland composed a poem that begins a series of aspirational poems written during the next few months that show him coming to grips with his grief. While it is not the purpose of this article to provide a psychological diagnosis of Ryland, it is not too much to say that these poems show Ryland

---

[65] To be fair, he does reference this common element of Christian union in Christ. He speaks in the poem of Noah hearing about Betsy's life with admiration and the new converts of Greenland rejoicing to converse with the Britons who are there (Ryland, *Poems*, 2:70). That is not Ryland's focus in the poem, however.

[66] Ryland, *Poems*, 2:71.

[67] Ryland, *Poems*, 2:70.

[68] When writing to his oldest son, John Tyler, before his own wedding day, Ryland emphasizes that aspect of the vows, writing in a poetic prayer:

> Protect his journey, Lord, to night,
> And let tomorrow's welcome light
> Pleasure before unknown impart;
> Fill both their hearts with sober bliss,
> Remembering, while they meet & kiss,
> That solemn Clause, "Till death shall part"
> (Ryland, *Poems*, 2:120).

to be in the midst of a spiritual desert from which he is seeking rescue.[69] The 26 February poem is relatively short and simple, a prayer for conformity to the likeness of Christ.[70]

The next poem was written several days later and is based on John 15:5, on which he preached the next day at College Lane in the morning.[71] In it, Ryland focuses on his sinfulness and need of Christ to override his passions and wickedness. He writes:

My heart is bad, deprav'd my Will,
My passions oft my reason blind;
I am perversly prone to Ill,
To Good I'm strangely disinclin'd.
I am all Badness, but thy Grace
My only Remedy I own;
Lord from my mind the darkness chase
And from my will remove the stone.[72]

Ryland's next entry in the poem book is dated 2 March 1788. Like the previous poems in this series, it is based on a text of Scripture from which he was to preach. In this case, it is Philippians 4:13, on which he preached that same day in the afternoon at College Lane. It is a curious poem. He dwells on Paul's claim that he can do all things through Christ. Much of the poem is depersonalized. Paul could claim that he could do all things through Christ, and even "The

---

[69] Indeed, in the previous months he had described himself as in a "dreary, desart Land" and praying for God to "refresh & cheer" his soul (Ryland, *Poems*, 2:59). The poems from this period demonstrate that he had not yet received a positive answer to that prayer.

[70] Ryland, *Poems*, 2:73:

Sure it is my chief desire
In thy likeness Lord to grow;
I wou'd constantly aspire
More of Jesus Christ to know;
So to know thee, as to be
Thoro'ly conform'd to thee.

[71] See Ryland, "Text Book," 2 March 1788.

[72] Ryland, *Poems*, 2:74. There is another dated 1 March 1788. It is based on 1 John 2:6, on which he preached the next day in the evening. It is less focused on sinfulness, but it is still aspirational. He is still striving for something he does not seem to possess. Ryland was clearly struggling spiritually at this time, with his state of mind described by Newton as a "thraldom" (John Newton, Letter to John Ryland, Jr., 30 April 1788, in Gordon, *Wise Counsel*, 205).

Christian Soldier" could claim this.⁷³ Of himself, however, Ryland only says:

> If I my weakness better knew
> And liv'd on Christ alone
> I in his strength cou'd all things do
> Paul cou'd not in his own.⁷⁴

Ryland seems to see himself as a poor follower of Christ, subsisting on his own strength and not that of Christ. While some of his expression here may be accounted for by his theological commitments, when placed in the context of the other poems written around the same time, it shows that Ryland, while still holding on to Christ in faith, could not claim to be walking in any sort of joy or peace of soul.⁷⁵ His faith was a hopeful faith, in the sense that he hoped one day to experience in his own life what he held to in faith.

The good news for the sympathetic reader of Ryland's poetry is that the next poem shows that the light was beginning once again to dawn for him. The poem is dated 5 April 1788, and it is based on 2 Chronicles 20:11–12, on which he preached on 27 April in the morning. It is the first where he speaks positively of himself and his spirituality. He says:

> Legions of Sins & Care & Fears
> My feeble Soul invade
> But when my blessed Lord appears
> His presence brings me aid.⁷⁶

It is a small stanza, but it speaks volumes in light of the struggles that have been evident in the poems since Betsy's death. He is still "feeble," but the Lord has begun to bring him aid by his presence, something he seems not to have enjoyed much in his recent past.

The next poem continues this theme of recovery. It is dated 3 June 1788, and it is based on Galatians 3:4 and was later published in the *Evangelical Magazine*.⁷⁷ He seems to be gaining perspective on his grief. He speaks of sharing in

---

⁷³ Ryland, *Poems*, 2:76.

⁷⁴ Ryland, *Poems*, 2:76.

⁷⁵ Ryland believed that human beings are wholly sinful. In the last piece he wrote for publication before he died, he writes of our "sinful and miserable condition," the presence of war as proof of "human depravity," and God's abiding treatment of the human race as guilty ("On the Alleged Impiety of Calvinism," *The Baptist Quarterly* [1825]: 278).

⁷⁶ Ryland, *Poems*, 2:77.

⁷⁷ This poem was published under the pen name "R." as "On Galatians, iii. 4," *Evangelical Magazine*

the sufferings of Jesus and the purpose of suffering:

> Of trials I meet by the way
> I wou'd not presume to complain
> But grant blessed Savior I may
> Not suffer so often in vain.[78]

The poem demonstrates an understanding of his suffering that is missing in prior poems. He is still not where he would like to be, but the darkness seems to be lifting from his life.[79] Indeed, the next poem reintroduces levity into Ryland's poetry. It is written to John Tyler and is, by Ryland's own admission, a bit silly:

> If the verse is but lame
> It may still wear the name
> As I only address it to you
> Papa sure may chat
> About this or that
> And good sense or nonsense will do
> I soon shall have done
> As it's only for fun
> That I write in this jingling way
> But if you cou'd talk
> As well as you walk
> I'd tell my dear boy what to say.[80]

Ryland then experiences what many who have mourned and then learned to laugh again after mourning: guilt. On 1 December 1788, "the second return of my ever dear Betsy's Birth day after her Glorification," he writes:[81]

(1795): 554. This poem is also unique in this time period in that it was not based on a passage on which he was soon to preach. He preached from Galatians 3:4 on 31 August 1788, which was almost two months later.

[78] Ryland, *Poems*, 2:78.

[79] He writes:
I long to be wholly thy own
Let Sin & let Self be subdued
Then Lord it shall clearly be shown
My Trials are working for good
(Ryland, *Poems*, 2:78).

[80] Ryland, *Poems*, 2:79.

[81] Ryland, *Poems*, 2:81.

Have I forgot her?—Judge me O <u>her</u> God!
I <u>court</u> the search of thine impartial Eye;
Thine eye which pierces hell's profound abode,
And all the earth surveys, & all the sky.[82]

For the rest of the poem, Ryland returns to a previous theme: God's sovereignty in Betsy's death. In this particular one, however, he leans most heavily on God's activity in taking Betsy but is also able to see how God had sustained him through "two years of worse than solitary Grief."[83]

Were I not conscious Thy unerring will
Had from my bosom torn that saint away,
Rivers of tears by night my bed wou'd fill,
And groans incessant wear out every day.
<u>Thou</u> Lord has done it—therefore I forbear,
Yes, <u>therefore only</u>, I my grief repress;
Else shou'd I be abandon'd to despair,
For sure my loss thou only canst redress.[84]

While he still could describe Betsy as an "earthly boon" he prized like no other, this poem also features the first mention of his second wife, Frances Barrett.[85] This first reference to the woman who would be his wife for thirty-six years is somewhat less impassioned than his references to Betsy.[86] He writes of Frances:

Yes, she has left a female friend behind
Who lov'd her much, was much by her belov'd,[87]

---

[82] Ryland, *Poems*, 2:81.

[83] Ryland, *Poems*, 2:82.

[84] Ryland, *Poems*, 2:81.

[85] Ryland, *Poems*, 2:81.

[86] Newton gives Ryland some intriguing advice around this time, saying, "As matters seem to have gone too far for receding with honour and propriety, and as you mean to marry in the Lord, I think you may trust him to give you such feelings as may suffice to make your relation comfortable" (John Newton, Letter to John Ryland, Jr., 20 January 1789, in Gordon, *Wise Counsel*, 214). It would seem as though Ryland was having second thoughts about his marriage to Frances.

[87] Betsy and Frances were indeed friends before Betsy's death. Ryland makes reference to this in several poems. In one written from the perspective of John Tyler, he writes:

My own dear Mother's friend

Of gentle Manners, & a kindred Mind,
A tender heart, & piety approv'd.
Grant me that friend to soothe Life's later Woes
And teach our infant Babe a Savior's Love
Till with my Betsy's Clay shall mine repose
And I shall join her in the Realms above.[88]

The poems of deep-rooted grief end with this one. Ryland and Frances Barrett were married on 18 June 1789, and it would seem that his prayer for comfort from Frances was answered positively. Ryland composed several poems with no references to Betsy, and the poems he did write were more joyful than those before. For example, on 31 July 1790, Ryland wrote a poem based on Psalm 45, on which he had preached several times around that time.[89] He writes:

Let us sing the King Messiah,
King of Righteousness & Peace;
Hail him all his happy Subjects,
Never let his praises cease:
Ever hail him,
Never let his praises cease.
How transcendent are thy Glories!
Fairer than the Sons of Men!

While thy blessed Mediation
Brings us back to God again
Blest Redeemer

Who lov'd her here below
And gladly will attend
To nurse & teach me now
(Ryland, *Poems*, 2:90).

In her diary, Frances records her own thoughts on Betsy: "The thought of presiding in the place of one I so dearly loved, and whose <u>temper</u> and <u>conduct</u> was so truly <u>amiable</u>, fills my heart with a thousand anxieties. No, I shall never forget the <u>sweetness of her love and esteem!</u> My hope is in God, otherwise the charge and care of her dear Infant, would occasion still greater concern. May the recollection of her kindness, affection, and sympathy, not only soften every care, but animate me to the <u>discharge</u> of <u>duties</u> how<u>ever</u> <u>difficult</u> <u>with all fidelity</u>" (Frances Barrett Ryland, *Spiritual Journal of MRS Ryland [1789–1806]*, [Bristol Baptist College Archives], 14 June 1789).

[88] Ryland, *Poems*, 2:81–83.

[89] Ryland, "Text Book," 22 July and 1 August 1790.

How we triumph in thy reign!⁹⁰

Theological poems such as this begin to be found once again in Ryland's book, mixed with more personal poems to his wife, children, and grandchildren.⁹¹ The references to Betsy slowly fade away. Ryland moves on, but he never forgot Betsy, the wife and love of his youth, for even decades after his death, in poems written to his second wife, Betsy makes the occasional appearance. Writing to Frances, his "dear Wife," in April 1808, Ryland mentions Betsy:⁹²

Her once you lov'd as well as I,
And now she waits, above the sky,
Our entrance there to greet;
In a few years before the throne,
In realms where sorrow is unknown
We shall her spirit meet.⁹³

Conclusion

It is not uncommon to find Calvinistic writers such as Ryland referring to the necessity of "kissing the rod" which struck them.⁹⁴ By this, they mean that they sought to understand the hand of God in their afflictions and accept it as their good. Ryland uses a form of it in the funeral sermon for his friend William Guy, telling the congregation, "Be humbled then under the rod of your heavenly Father, and enquire, Was there not a cause for this stroke?"⁹⁵ He would later

---

⁹⁰ Ryland, *Poems*, 2:92. This poem was published under the pen name "R." as "Success to the Arms of Messiah," *Evangelical Magazine* 1 (1793): 44. It has since been put to use as a hymn, appearing in numerous hymnals in the nineteenth and twentieth centuries, such as *Missionary Hymns, Composed and Selected for the Public Services at the Annual Meetings of the Missionary Society, in London* (London: W. Arding, 1814), No. 23; *The Hymnary: For Use in Baptist Churches* (Whitby, ON: Ryerson Press, 1936), No. 10; *Hymns of Hope: Founded on the Psalms and the New Covenant* (London: Elliot Stock, 1879), No. 328; *Baptist Praise and Worship* (New York: Oxford University Press, 1991), No. 631.

⁹¹ Ryland had three daughters, Elizabeth Barrett Ryland, Frances Barrett Ryland, and Mary Ryland. He also had another son, Jonathan Edwards Ryland. Curiously, no poems survive that were written to Jonathan Edwards Ryland.

⁹² Ryland, *Poems*, 2:36.

⁹³ Ryland, *Poems*, 2:36–37.

⁹⁴ See, for example, John Bunyan, *Seasonable Counsel: Or, Advice to Sufferers* (London: Benjamin Alsop, 1684), 62; John Newton, *The Christian Correspondent; or a Series of Religious Letters* (Hull: George Prince, 1790), 158; and James Hervey, *Letters from the Late Reverend James Hervey, A.M., Rector of Weston Flavel to the Right Honourable Lady Frances Shirley* (London: John Rivington, 1782), 273. The phrase was not limited to Calvinist or even religious literature. Shakespeare used it in *Richard II*, 5.1.32.

⁹⁵ John Ryland, *Seasonable Hints to a Bereaved Church; and the Blessedness of the Dead, Who Die in*

exhort another congregation at a funeral service with these words: "To consider the Hand of God in our Afflictions is the Way to calm our Minds, which are too ready to fret at Instruments & 2^d Causes, & overlook the first. By this we often miss the Benefit of Afflict^s. even when we do not directly fret ag^t. God himself."[96]

What Ryland's poems show is that giving these kinds of exhortations is somewhat easier than obeying them. The calming of the mind and realizing the benefits of affliction, of which Ryland wrote, do not happen overnight and may, in fact, come only after a long struggle. The poems show that the men whose well-edited books and sermons that historians study sometimes walked with a spiritual and psychological limp.

---

the Lord (Northampton: T. Dicey, 1783), 21.

[96] John Ryland, "Sermon Notes: Job 1:21," *Original Manuscript Sermons: Old Testament, Vol. I* (Bristol Baptist College Archives, Bristol Baptist College, Bristol).

Andrew Fuller and the biblical languages: An exception that proves the rule

Chad C. Ashby

Chad C. Ashby is a graduate of The Southern Baptist Theological Seminary (M.Div., Biblical & Theological Studies) and Grove City College. He currently is the pastor at College Street Baptist Church in Newberry, SC.

In a 1524 treatise addressed to German city councilmen, Martin Luther (1483–1546) implores his readers to see the value of studying and knowing the languages of the Scriptures. In fact, he pushes his argument so far as to say, "Let us be sure of this: we will not long preserve the gospel without the languages."[1] To Luther, Greek and Hebrew were the keys to unlocking the good news of Jesus Christ; without them it was impossible to retain the truth. Later in the same treatise Luther insists that the preacher who is "versed in the languages" has a "freshness and vigor to his preaching" such that "faith finds itself constantly renewed."[2] Luther pleads with his audience to understand that the church is continually in need of men who have the tools to dig deep into the scriptures. Luther understood that not all men are gifted to be technical expositors—or prophets, as he calls them. He willingly admits, "A simple preacher (it is true) has so many clear passages and texts available through translations that he can know and teach Christ."[3] However, the unlearned preacher has his limitations: "When it comes to interpreting Scripture … and disputing with those who cite

---

[1] Martin Luther, "To the Councilmen of All Cities in Germany That They Establish and Maintain Christian Schools" in *Luther's Works*, ed. W. Brandt and H. Lehman (Philadelphia, PA: Muhlenberg Press, 1962), 45:363.

[2] Luther, "To the Councilmen of All Cities in Germany" in *Luther's Works*, 45:366.

[3] Luther, "To the Councilmen of All Cities in Germany" in *Luther's Works*, 45:366.

it incorrectly, he is unequal to the task; that cannot be done without the languages."[4]

Though Luther's statements have been borne out in the lives of Christian theologians and pastors throughout the centuries, one man stands as a blatant contradiction to all that Luther claims: Andrew Fuller (1754–1815). Known for his prowess in disputation with enemies of the gospel, his genuine and Christ-centered preaching, and his wisdom and insight with regards to scripture, this turn-of-the-nineteenth-century Particular Baptist had no further education than the common rudiments of English education offered at the free school in Soham.[5] The school, located in a community whose members struggled to scrape together the paltry salary of thirteen pounds a year for their local minister, was undoubtedly of humble quality.[6] Moreover, Fuller entered his ministry at quite a young age—and without any formal training. Nevertheless, a contemporary author bestowed this high praise upon Fuller's preaching: "You are surprised at and seem to have found a man in whom are united the clearness of Barrow, the scriptural theology of [John] Owen [1616–1683], and the subduing tenderness of [Richard] Baxter [1615–1691] or [John] Flavel [ca.1627–1691]."[7]

Though Fuller himself was not destined by divine providence to become a man of exegetical and critical stature like his contemporary John Gill (1697–1771), he accomplished quite an opus of theological and pastoral work for the profit of Christians in his day and thereafter, not without the help of the original languages. He was far from skilled in either Greek or Hebrew, but he made efforts during his life to become acquainted with both. Additionally, he was not afraid to broach discussion on the technicalities of the text in his writings when the occasion arose. Fuller also developed a theology which assigned, in his mind, a proper place for critical reading of the text among the disciplines of the pastor-theologian.

Fuller's grasp of the languages
There is more than enough convincing evidence that Fuller did have some knowledge of both Greek and Hebrew, but it is more difficult to establish to

---

[4] Luther, "To the Councilmen of All Cities in Germany" in *Luther's Works*, 45:366.

[5] J.W. Morris, *Memoirs of the Life and Writings of Andrew Fuller* (Boston: Lincoln & Edmands, 1830), 13.

[6] John Ryland, Jr., *The Life and Death of Andrew Fuller* (London: Button & Son, Paternoster Row, 1816), 71.

[7] An editorial comment from Joseph Belcher found in *The Complete Works of the Rev. Andrew Fuller*, ed. Andrew Gunton Fuller, revised Joseph Belcher, 3rd ed. (1845, Harrisonburg, VA: Sprinkle Publications, 1988), 1:107.

what extent he was—or was not—skilled in expositing from the original texts. The perspectives of his contemporaries and friends are helpful in evaluating his abilities. In addition, Fuller left behind some interesting paper trails that help to establish the breadth of his knowledge in Greek and Hebrew.

An outsider assessment of Fuller's abilities
Fuller's son Andrew Gunton Fuller (1799–1884) includes several remarks about his father's scholarly attainments in his *Memoir*. He makes plain, "Mr. Fuller made no pretensions to scholarship, or to the graces of composition."[8] Yet, his father possessed such a "clear, nervous grip of the English language," which shined brightest when one of his opponents brought forth distinctions or terms that required accuracy and acuity of speech.[9] Readers of Fuller will undoubtedly concur with the younger Fuller's assessment of the quickness of wit and precision that characterized his controversial publications. It would seem that Fuller had an intrinsic, keen eye for detail which would be necessary for careful study of the languages of Scripture.[10] Andrew Gunton Fuller comments as much: "He was far less indebted to early training than to his native perspicacity and strong sense."[11]

The *Memoir* contains more specific details regarding Fuller's abilities in biblical criticism. A large portion of Fuller's works deal with the careful exposition of Scripture, and A.G. Fuller marvels that his father "attained to a more than common measure of its [biblical criticism's] results with a very small amount of literary qualification."[12] The younger Fuller is implying that in his estimation, his father did not have a strong grasp on the tools with which one typical performed biblical criticism: Greek and Hebrew. However, he admires his father's vast accomplishments; it is as though Fuller managed to plow an entire three-hundred-acre field using only a hand trowel. A.G. Fuller mentions that his father was aided by his friend John Ryland Jr(1753–1825) in developing some skills in this area of study.[13]

Another of Fuller's acquaintances, his publisher John Webster Morris (1763–1836), writes about Fuller's abilities as an expositor. He praises Fuller

---

[8] Andrew Gunton Fuller, "Memoir" in *Complete Works of Andrew Fuller*, 1:167.

[9] Fuller, "Memoir" in *Complete Works of Andrew Fuller*, 1:167.

[10] T. David Gordon, a media ecologist, comments, "The highly inflected nature of classical languages creates an attentiveness to grammatical detail that causes an individual to be very precise" (Gordon, *Why Johnny Can't Preach: The Media Have Shaped the Messengers* [Phillipsburg, PA: P&R, 2009], 40).

[11] Fuller, "Memoir" in *Complete Works of Andrew Fuller*, 1:167.

[12] Fuller, "Memoir" in *Complete Works of Andrew Fuller*, 1:167.

[13] Fuller, "Memoir" in *Complete Works of Andrew Fuller*, 1:167.

for his talent at sounding the depths of a text, finding its place in the analogy of faith, and applying it to his hearers with conviction to the heart.[14] Fuller was not one to become caught up in the vagaries of unclear inferences and imaginary notions with regards to the texts of the Bible. Morris notes that expounding the scriptures much delighted Fuller, but he did not "undertake any thing like a critical exposition, nor did he profess himself a critic on any subject."[15] Fuller never claimed to be an expert in the languages, nor are any of his writings pure critical commentary in nature. Morris is correct when he writes, "Indeed, he had no great liking to the generality of critical commentators."[16] Fuller's experience with the Sandemanians and other opponents who claimed to be experts at expositing the original languages produced in him a negative disposition toward most critical scholarship.

One final example is found in Francis Augustus Cox (1783–1853), Fuller's co-laborer in the Baptist Mission Society. In his *History of the Baptist Mission Society*, Cox includes a sly remark about Fuller, "he had not, like [William] Carey [1761–1834], to use a favourite phrase of his own, a *turn* for languages."[17] Carey, who was engaged in Bible translation from the original languages, was much more skilled than Fuller. Though Fuller had not been schooled formally in the languages, he made some headway nonetheless: "He applied to them with some success, so as to be able to understand the Greek Testament."[18] Cox provides a more specific assessment than the first two accounts given; he establishes certainty that Fuller had a grasp on New Testament Greek. Fuller came to understand some of the merits of reading the Bible in this way, but, Cox writes, "He was not attracted by the study, and had he even possessed leisure, probably would never have pursued it to any great extent."[19]

The extent of Fuller's pursuit of the languages
Returning to A.G. Fuller's memoir, there are some interesting comments about what he found among his father's belongings after his death. He writes about a small elementary Hebrew book that he discovered with Fuller's papers; with it were copies of the first and twenty-third Psalms written in Hebrew. A.G. Fuller is certain that "the doctor," that is Ryland, was the one who wrote these

---

[14] Morris, *Memoirs*, 71–72.

[15] Morris, *Memoirs*, 71.

[16] Morris, *Memoirs*, 71.

[17] F.A. Cox, *History of the Baptist Mission Society* (London: T. Ward & Co., and G. & J. Dyer, 1842), 1:266.

[18] Cox, *History*, 1:266.

[19] Cox, *History*, 1:266.

copies out for Fuller because he recognized "the unrivalled beauty of penmanship characteristic of him."[20] Fuller's close friend John Ryland must have been aiding him in his pursuit of Hebrew at some point in his life. A.G. Fuller also references another memorandum-book in which Fuller demonstrates his proficiency at writing Hebrew characters, and he cites Fuller's disputations with Dan Taylor (1738–1816) as demonstration of Fuller's abilities in the language.[21] Furthermore, he also comments that he found a book in Fuller's handwriting that contained "elements of Greek."[22]

Fuller and the Hebrew language
One such book that A.G. Fuller found among his father's papers has been obtained by The Southern Baptist Theological Seminary. This handwritten manuscript is an early draft of Fuller's famous work *The Gospel Worthy of All Acceptation*.[23] What is of interest to this study is the later work Fuller performed on the backsides of these pages. Beginning on the last page of this book, Fuller has written the title page, "*Hebrew Grammar* by Israel Lyons."[24] From this, Fuller seems to have begun to copy pages out of this grammar onto the backsides of the pages of his composition book.[25] What is more, on other back pages in this book, Fuller catalogs some of his library. In a list entitled "Duodecimo Pamphlets Sep. 92," item nineteen is entitled "*Hebrew Grammar*," and for item thirty-eight is written "*Excellency of Hebrew Language.*" What is clear from this source is that Fuller had resources for learning Hebrew in his library some time before September 1792.

Further evidence of Fuller's work in the language of the Old Testament can be found on the backsides of the front pages of this manuscript. In a two-page section, the title "Robertson 12 + 3, 12 Chapter Isaiah" appears above a chart

---

[20] Fuller, "Memoir" in *Complete Works of Andrew Fuller*, 1:167.

[21] Fuller, "Memoir" in *Complete Works of Andrew Fuller*, 1:167.

[22] Fuller, "Memoir" in *Complete Works of Andrew Fuller*, 1:167.

[23] Andrew Fuller, *Thoughts on the Power of Men to do the Will of God*, MS (Special Collections Archives, Southern Baptist Theological Seminary, Louisville, KY). In a letter written by A.G. Fuller that was enclosed in the cover of the journal's binding, he calls the book a "manuscript of his early life," and he claims it was written in 1777 or 1778, when Fuller was twenty-three or twenty-four. This leaflet is catalogued together with *Thoughts on the Power* in the Special Collections Archives at SBTS.

[24] Fuller, *Thoughts on the Power of Men to do the Will of God*.

[25] According to William Nicholson in *The British Encyclopedia Dictionary* (Whittingham: Mitchell Ames and White, 1809), 4:43, Israel Lyons was a Jewish teacher at Cambridge who wrote *The Scholar's Instructor or Hebrew Grammar*, which was published in a second edition in 1757.

consisting of columns with various headings.²⁶ On this chart Fuller writes out each Hebrew word beginning at verse 1, its English pronunciation, his translation, the verbal root, and the root's translation. Another backside of a page bears the inscription "Tryals" and is dated "July 10, [1]803." This page is Fuller's attempt at translating Genesis 1.²⁷ He translates verses 1 through the beginning of verse 6 where he quits mid-sentence.²⁸ In the midst of his translation, it is clear that he is using some sort of lexicon, because he inserts a parenthetical aside containing an entry concerning the word *moved* in verse 2: "a violent tremulous motion; to flatten out, to agitate in order; excite what is sluggish & inactive."²⁹ These two sections of exercises show that Fuller was making attempts to grow in his knowledge of Hebrew. He was at one time able to translate portions of Genesis and Isaiah—of this one can be sure.

Fuller and the Greek language
Cox's comments as previously mentioned assert from without that Fuller was competent to understand much of the Greek New Testament. Fuller's writings are also a testimony to a certain depth of understanding when it came to the original language of the New Testament. However, two instances are presented here for investigation. In his work *The Reality and Efficacy of Divine Grace*, Letter XII, Fuller debates Dan Taylor who has argued that Fuller mistranslates 2 Corinthians 5:14. Fuller then inserts the Greek text under dispute: "The words of the apostle are, ὅτι εἰ εἷς ὑπὲρ πάντον ἀπέθανεν, ἄρα οἱ πάντες ἀπέθανον."³⁰ Poking fun at his opponent, Fuller sarcastically admits that he was not forward enough to claim "to be able to judge of the propriety of a translation."³¹ Yet, he believes that he has the support of some "very competent judges* [Theodore Beza (1519–1605), Johannes Piscator (1546–1625), and John Gill]" when he asserts that the article οἱ in the passage is anaphoric or relative.³² Thus, Fuller is

---

²⁶ Fuller, *Thoughts on the Power of Men to do the Will of God*. Fuller was certainly working through William Robertson, *The First Gate or the Outward Door to the Holy Tongue, Opened in English* (United Kingdom: University of Edinburgh, 1654), 121ff. This short primer contains various charts followed by three sections translating portions of Obadiah, the Decalogue, and Isaiah Chapter 12.

²⁷ Fuller, *Thoughts on the Power of Men to do the Will of God*.

²⁸ The date of this translation makes one wonder whether he began it as an attempt in conjunction with his *Expository Discourses on The Book of Genesis* which was published in late 1805, only two years after the dating of these "Tryals."

²⁹ Fuller, *Thoughts on the Power of Men to do the Will of God*.

³⁰ Andrew Fuller, *The Reality and Efficacy of Divine Grace* in *Complete Works of Andrew Fuller*, 2:553.

³¹ Fuller, *The Reality and Efficacy of Divine Grace* in *Complete Works of Andrew Fuller*, 2:553.

³² Fuller, *The Reality and Efficacy of Divine Grace* in *Complete Works of Andrew Fuller*, 2:553.

quite familiar with grammatical terms dealing with the Greek article; his willingness to enter the arena of Greek criticism with his opponent also indicates his comfort level with the material.

Finally, an interesting footnote in one of Fuller's collected sermons raises an interesting question. In the piece entitled "Hope in the Last Extremity" contained in the *Sermons and Sketches*, Fuller makes reference to "[John] Parkhurst's [1728–1797] Greek Lexicon, on κητος."[33] What is curious about this footnote is the fact that Fuller is expounding upon Jonah 2:4, and the footnote is with reference to the word typically translated "fish." Therefore, it is possible that Fuller was consulting with a source containing the Septuagint text of Jonah 2. At least, Fuller is able to navigate his way through a concordance that connects the Hebrew of the Old Testament with the Septuagint. In any case, Fuller further reveals the extent of his skills with regards to the Greek language.

Fuller's interaction with the biblical languages in his writings
A man's writings are often a good gauge of his comfort level on a certain subject. No respectable writer is willing to go on the record about something he has little to no knowledge about, else he be made a fool in the eyes of the experts. Andrew Fuller was not an author who frequently referenced the original languages in his works; this alone indicates his own assessment of his lack of abilities. However, the acumen and competency he displays when he allows his opponents to coax him into the arena of biblical criticism betrays a hint of self-deprecation. There are two primary texts that showcase Fuller's abilities.

Fuller's Expository Discourses on the Book of Genesis.
In the discourse of Fuller's work on Genesis 1, he reveals his work in the original languages. He explains to his readers that the writer of Genesis uses "the plural term *Elohim*, which yet is joined to singular verbs."[34] He goes on to assert that this is the first indication of plurality in the unity of the Godhead. In conjunction with this statement he brings forth verse 26 and its use of first person plural pronouns when God refers to himself.[35] It is possible that Fuller found this explanation from a commentary without studying the original text; however, it was established earlier that Fuller himself practiced translating these very verses.[36] The likelihood is that he translated from the Hebrew to establish

---

[33] Andrew Fuller, "Hope in the Last Extremity" in *Complete Works of Andrew Fuller*, 1:457.

[34] Andrew Fuller, *Expository Discourses on the Book of Genesis* in *Complete Works of Andrew Fuller*, 3:2–3.

[35] Fuller, *Expository Discourses on the Book of Genesis* in *Complete Works of Andrew Fuller*, 3:3.

[36] See previous section and discussion on the contents of the manuscript, *Thoughts on the Power of Men to Do the Will of God*. It is true that Fuller is probably consulting Matthew Henry's (1662–1714) *Commen-*

these facts for himself before putting them before his readers.

Further evidence supports this connection between Fuller's "Tryals" and his *Expository Discourses on the Book of Genesis* when his comments on verse 2 are considered. In both his published work and his unpublished translation, he emphasizes the word "moved"—in the one it is written *moved* and in the latter, it is underlined, "moved."[37] Interestingly, he provides a similar lexical description of the Hebrew word used here in both his published and unpublished version of the text. Therefore, it is likely that he was working through these Hebrew exercises at a time similar to his studies for writing his expositions on the text. What is curious is that in the same way that Fuller's translation exercises abruptly stopped in the middle of verse 6, Fuller's careful attention to the technicalities of the original language in his *Expository Discourses* also ceases abruptly at the close of the first discourse never to resume for the rest of the work.

Fuller's Letters to Mr. Vidler
Perhaps nowhere else in the corpus of Fuller's works is his ability to understand and reason through the original languages more evident than in his response in Letter VI to William Vidler (1758–1816), a Socinian pastor from Battle, East Sussex.[38] Vidler has presented Fuller with an extensive argument against eternal punishment that hinges upon technicalities in Hebrew and Greek. Fuller acknowledges this fact by saying, "I thought that you as well as myself, had better not have attempted to criticize on Hebrew and Greek terms. You think otherwise. Very well."[39] Fuller is not afraid to follow his opponent's lead. Fuller states that he knows עלם, the Hebrew word rendered "everlasting" to which Vidler refers, and he has done a concordance study on all of its occurrences to discern its meaning.[40] Continuing in his response, he sarcastically derides Vidler for presenting him with an elementary lesson on the meaning of the Greek words αἰὼν and αἰώνιος.[41]

---

tary on the Whole Bible; if one consults the similarities between some of Fuller's exposition of verses 1–3 and Henry's comments, it is clear that Fuller must be borrowing some language from this resource.

[37] Fuller, *Expository Discourses on the Book of Genesis* in *Complete Works of Andrew Fuller*, 3:3; Fuller, *Thoughts on the Power of Men to do the Will of God*.

[38] On Vidler, see F.W. Butt-Thompson, "William Vidler," *Baptist Quarterly* 17, no.1 (1957): 3–9; F.W. Butt-Thompson, *The History of the Battle Baptist Church: With a Biography of William Vidler, Baptist & Universalist, Its First Pastor* (Hastings, East Sussex: Burfield & Pennells, 1909).

[39] Andrew Fuller, *Letters to Mr. Vidler* in *Complete Works of Andrew Fuller*, 2:314.

[40] Fuller, *Letters to Mr. Vidler* in *Complete Works of Andrew Fuller*, 2:313.

[41] Fuller, *Letters to Mr. Vidler* in *Complete Works of Andrew Fuller*, 2:314.

Fuller then plunges into a deeply technical discussion on the interaction of English and Greek when translating from one language to another. It is as though he senses the true weakness of his opponent in the area of biblical criticism, and he is a shark circling for the kill. He then cites the original Greek from Ephesians 2:11 and 1 Timothy 1:17, providing his own translations of the texts.[42] After this argument, Fuller states his conclusion, "The Greek words αἰὼν and αἰώνιος are no less expressive of endless duration than the English words *everlasting* and *eternal*."[43] Having made a mockery of Vidler's biblical criticism with his own logic and understanding of the original Greek, Fuller finishes off the section with a flourish. If his conclusion is true, then the arguments of Vidler and his fellows "*is no better than a sing-song; a mere affection of learning, serving to mislead the ignorant.*"[44] In the conclusion of his letter, Fuller claims that he is not "pretending to any thing like a critical knowledge of either the Greek or Hebrew language;" yet Fuller's confidence in the face of an opponent displays his level of comfort with regards to discussing the original languages.[45]

Fuller's perspective on the value and usefulness of the languages
In Fuller's mind, the languages were secondary; they were meant to serve other primary purposes. Knowledge or critical use of the original languages was never an end to itself. He speaks to the place of original languages in four primary areas of the pastor-theologian's life: preaching, debate and writing, missions and bible translation, and clarity of Scripture.

Preaching
Fuller was not one to use his pulpit to engage in controversy or squabbles over technicalities; it was a place to proclaim the gospel of Christ. His biographer, Morris characterizes Fuller's pulpit ministry in this way: "*There* he took the high places of the field; *here* he tarried at home and divided the spoil. The least disputable points of religion, which are at all times the most essential, were the leading theme of his ministry."[46] For Fuller, the preacher must bring to his people a clear and concise message; it was his duty as a minister "to understand every part of Scripture, in order to explain it to the people."[47]

Sermon preparation for Fuller did not typically involve any study in the

---

[42] Fuller, *Letters to Mr. Vidler* in *Complete Works of Andrew Fuller*, 2:313.

[43] Fuller, *Letters to Mr. Vidler* in *Complete Works of Andrew Fuller*, 2:314.

[44] Fuller, *Letters to Mr. Vidler* in *Complete Works of Andrew Fuller*, 2:315.

[45] Fuller, *Letters to Mr. Vidler* in *Complete Works of Andrew Fuller*, 2:318.

[46] Morris, *Memoirs*, 69.

[47] Andrew Fuller, *Thoughts on Preaching* in *Complete Works of Andrew Fuller*, 1:712.

original languages. Morris insists that composing his sermons was the easiest part of Fuller's ministry, and it generally took an hour or two at the close of the week. Indeed, if he was quite pressed for time, he would sometimes prepare sermons between services on the Sabbath.[48] In his brief article "Thoughts on Preaching," Fuller challenges young ministers not to become bogged down with word studies or investigations into technicalities: "The scope of the sacred writers is of greater importance in understanding the Scriptures than the most critical examination of terms."[49] If the minister is to spend his time wisely, he will seek to read and comprehend the depths of scripture and will leave behind concordances and criticism. For Fuller, this meant that the languages played almost no role in his pulpit or sermon preparation.[50]

Debate and writing
Fuller constantly emphasized the importance of coming to the scriptures with an open heart and mind. According to Fuller, many of his opponents were "acquainted with the original languages, and able to criticize texts; and yet [could] not discern the mind of the Spirit."[51] What was at issue was that they came to the text with a system of preconceived doctrines through which they read the scriptures. A man who comes to the scriptures in this manner is like Thomas Paine (1737–1809), who Fuller states, "reads the Scriptures to pervert and vilify them."[52] For this reason, Fuller tended to decry the use of biblical criticism among his opponents because they used it for ill purposes.

In "Veneration for the Scriptures" from Fuller's work, *The Calvinistic and Socinian Systems Examined and Compared*, Fuller takes his Socinian opponents to task for their abusive use of the original languages. These men employed their knowledge of Hebrew and Greek to twist the meaning of texts; they "mangled and altered the translation to their own minds, informing us that such a term *may* be rendered so."[53] Fuller was wary of any debate that made use of re-translating texts of Scripture so as to support one's claims. Though he admits translations are imperfect and open to constant revision, Fuller asserts,

---

[48] Morris, *Memoirs*, 70.

[49] Fuller, *Complete Works of Andrew Fuller*, 1:713.

[50] This is merely a statement of a fact. It is up to the reader to determine the validity of Fuller as an example for proper sermon preparation.

[51] Andrew Fuller, "The Satisfaction Derived from Godly Simplicity" in *Complete Works of Andrew Fuller*, 1:540.

[52] Fuller, "The Satisfaction Derived from Godly Simplicity" in *Complete Works of Andrew Fuller*, 1:540.

[53] Andrew Fuller, Letter XII "Veneration for the Scriptures" of *The Calvinistic and Socinian Systems Examined and Compared, as to Their Moral Tendency* in *Complete Works of Andrew Fuller*, 2:205.

"Where alterations are made by those who have an end to answer by them, they ought always to be suspected."[54] Fuller was highly suspicious of arguments that balanced upon criticism in the original languages; he would rather that men dispute over a commonly held translation than that they each establish their own translation from which to dispute. In his arguments with the Socinians, Fuller became fed up with this tendency: "In short, if we must never quote Scripture except according to the rules imposed upon us by Socinian writers, we must not quote it at all."[55] Fuller believed that the original languages were best left on the sideline when debating an opponent, though it was demonstrated in the previous section that he was willing and able to answer his opponents' arguments when they insisted on dragging Hebrew and Greek terms into discussion.

Missions and Bible translation

Fuller was a driving force behind the Baptist Mission Society, and he understood the need for translations of the scriptures into indigenous languages. When writing of Fuller's role in this organization, Cox explains that although Fuller was not particularly gifted in translation, "he had a mind and a heart to appreciate the literary efforts of others."[56] Fuller insists that some Christian men will be gifted by the Spirit and qualified to work in the original languages. These men ought to become part of societies, some of which would "translate the sacred Scriptures into the languages of the nations," while others would "teach the rising generation to read and write."[57] Scripture translation was a necessary part of missions, and for this purpose Fuller commended men with such a gifting in Hebrew and Greek.

Clarity of Scripture and personal enrichment

Fuller fully promoted and endorsed the careful understanding of the texts of scripture. Though much of his writings and discourses seem to demean the use of the original languages, he openly states, "It is not of criticizing, and much less of judiciously explaining the Scriptures, that [I complain], but of perverting them."[58] Fuller was not so gifted, but he encouraged those who were able to

---

[54] Fuller, *Calvinistic and Socinian Systems Examined and Compared* in *Complete Works of Andrew Fuller*, 2:205.

[55] Fuller, *Calvinistic and Socinian Systems Examined and Compared* in *Complete Works of Andrew Fuller*, 2:205.

[56] Cox, *History*, 1:266.

[57] Andrew Fuller, "The Increase of Knowledge" in *Complete Works of Andrew Fuller*, 1:419.

[58] Andrew Fuller, "Reflection on Mr. Belsham's Review of Mr. Wilberforce's *Treatise on Christianity*" in *Complete Works of Andrew Fuller*, 2:290.

use the original languages to lay plain the meaning of scripture. In fact, Fuller encourages ministers to intensely wrestle with the texts of scripture and not to become dependent upon critical commentators: "A small portion obtained by our own labour is sweeter than a large inheritance bequeathed by our predecessors."[59] For those more capable in Hebrew or Greek than Fuller, this might mean spending time grappling with the original texts of the Bible.

Conclusion
When Fuller recognized an aptitude and astuteness in his nephew Joseph Fuller (1778–1812), he was quick to see him schooled by his "friend Mr. Mason, of Rowell."[60] At home on a winter holiday, Joseph picked up the Greek alphabet on a whim. Upon his return, Fuller contacted the Rev. Mr. Brotherhood who happily agreed to mentor the young man in Latin and Greek languages free of charge. From 1807 and 1808, it was Joseph's habit to walk to the neighboring town of Desborough after his school lessons to receive an hour's instruction from the generous Mr. Brotherhood.[61] Fuller and Ryland believed this young man "looked to have a promising career in ministry."[62]

Perhaps Fuller's desire was to give Joseph more advantages with regards to the original languages than he had as a young man entering the ministry. Though he never experienced formal training in Greek or Hebrew, it is quite evident that Fuller made efforts to improve at both, and he was able to converse with those who did employ it in their writings. The languages only tend to appear in his own works in response to critical claims of his opponents. Fuller always saw the attainment of the languages as a subservient tool that must be put to proper use by those who wield it. Fuller's own statement is quite apt: "These are a part of the weapons of our warfare; but it is through God that they become mighty to the pulling down of strong holds."[63]

---

[59] Andrew Fuller, "Reading the Scriptures" in *Complete Works of Andrew Fuller*, 3:789.

[60] Fuller, *Memoirs* in *Complete Works of Andrew Fuller*, 1:93. Rothwell, alternately known as "Rowell," and Desborough are two miles from one another located northwest of Kettering in Northamptonshire. Fuller is referring to his friends William Brotherhood and William Mason.

[61] Fuller, *Memoirs* in *Complete Works of Andrew Fuller*, 1:93.

[62] Ryland, *Memoirs*, 13.

[63] Fuller, *Thoughts on Preaching* in *Complete Works of Andrew Fuller*, 1:717.

Texts & documents

"The sum and quintessence of all our bliss": a letter of Anne Dutton[1]

Edited by Michael A.G. Haykin

Michael A.G. Haykin is Chair and Professor of Church History and Director, The Andrew Fuller Center for Baptist Studies at The Southern Baptist Theological Seminary, Louisville, Kentucky.

Introduction
The recipients of this letter from Anne Dutton (1692–1765) are unknown. They have evidently experienced a great loss, though what they have lost is not specified. It does not appear to have been a person, but more likely property or wealth. The advice—to find their wealth in God their Father—is classic Dutton. The allusion to one of the letters of the Puritan author Samuel Rutherford (ca. 1600–1661) is a good indication of the roots of Dutton's piety, many of which were to be found in Puritan literature.

Text
Dear brother and sister,   1740
May the peace of God that passeth all understanding keep your hearts and minds through Christ Jesus.

I am exceedingly glad that you are helped to bear your loss patiently; believing that the Lord will do you good by it. Our dear Father never takes any good thing from us, but in order to give us something better. He has taken away

---

[1] This text was printed as a letter in *The Christian's Monthly Record* (London, 1881): 81. Capitalization has been modernized.

your pebbles to give you pearls; emptied you of riches in show to fill you with true riches and never-failing substance. Bless him, therefore, for taking as well as for giving.[2] His love cast the lot this way.[3] A little grace is better than much gold. You will be great gainers by your loss, if the Lord give you submission to his sovereign disposal under it, acquiescence with his good pleasure in it, and a further acquaintance with himself as your everlasting All by it. Mr. Rutherford calls the world, "the clay-portion of bastards; not the inheritance of the children."[4]

It is a great thing for a saint that is rich in this world to be thoroughly sensible of its nothingness, and to live beside his outward enjoyment upon that infinite, inexhaustible fulness he has in God. The creatures stand as a blind between us and him. And God loves his children so that he claims our hearts; and rather than lack them, he will strike the creatures dead, that himself, the life of all our joys, might be exceedingly endeared to us. He will dry up the streams of creature-comforts, that our thirsty souls may learn to drink their fill at the Fountain-head.[5] And so great is his grace that it pleaseth him well to make his children come to his bosom for all they want, when starved out of creature supplies!

O what fools are we to catch at shadows and let go the substance, the sum and quintessence of all our bliss! O how happy should we be if infinite sweetness did always ravish our souls, and mark out us from all the creatures! O the crystal streams which proceed out of the throne of God, and of the Lamb![6] How sweet are they at the Well-Head! What a pure river of water of life should we swim in could we always live in God! This will be our life in heaven, to the utmost perfection; and happy they who are aspiring after the rising glory, and highest degree of it here on earth!

The Father of mercies and God of all comforts fill you with all joy and peace in believing!

      I am, yours in Christ for ever,
      One who has tasted that the Lord is gracious.

---

[2] Job 1:21.

[3] Proverbs 16:33.

[4] This appears to be Dutton's paraphrase, for in his letter to the Lady Cardonness the Elder, Rutherford wrote, "Let not the world be your portion: What have ye to do with dead clay? Ye are not a bastard but a lawful begotten child; therefore set your heart on the inheritance" (*Joshua Redivivus, Or Mr. Rutherfoord's Letters, Divided into Two Parts* [Rotterdam, 1664], 348–349, modernized).

[5] Psalm 42:1–2; John 4:13–14; Revelation 7:16–17.

[6] Revelation 22:1.

Consolation in spiritual darkness: A letter from Daniel Turner to Benjamin Beddome 1762

Edited by Gary Brady

Gary Brady, ThM, has been pastor of Childs Hill Baptist Church, London, since 1983.

In 1815, *The Baptist Quarterly* reproduced a letter that had been written over forty years before from one Baptist minister and hymn writer to another. The following year this letter was reproduced as a separate tract by a leading Independent minister George Burder (1752–1832) with the title, *Consolation in Spiritual Darkness*. Burder comments that the letter "seems to be so well calculated to relieve a conscience burdened with guilt that I recommended the publication of it as a separate tract."[1]

The recipient of the letter was Benjamin Beddome (1717–1795). A son of the manse, Beddome was born in Henley-in-Arden, Warwickshire, but grew up in Bristol. After his pastoral training in Bristol and London, Beddome became the pastor of the Baptist Church in Burton-on-the-Water (in the Cotswolds, Gloucestershire) in 1640. Being a frequent speaker at the annual meetings of the Midland Baptist Association, and despite more than one call from other churches, Beddome remained in Bourton for the rest of his life. Many of his sermons were published posthumously but he is remembered today, if at all, chiefly for his hymns.

---

[1] Daniel Turner, *Consolation in Spiritual Darkness: A Letter* (London: J. Dennett, 1816). It also appeared in the July 1862 issue of *The Sower* where the editor inexplicably credits it to the Puritan divine Thomas Brooks (1608–1680). It also appeared in *The Gospel Magazine* in 1800 and 1850.

The writer of the letter was Daniel Turner (1710–1798), who was slightly older than Beddome.[2] Turner was born in Hertfordshire at Blackwater Farm, near St. Albans, and was taught in Hemel Hempstead by a pastor called Dr. James. Turner himself went on to keep a boarding school in Hemel Hempstead for a short while. He also acted as a visiting preacher at local Baptist chapels and in 1741 became the pastor of the Baptist church in Reading, which is in the neighbouring county of Berkshire. In 1748, he moved to nearby Abingdon, today in Oxfordshire, where he remained until his death. Bourton belonged to the Midland Association but Abingdon to the east belonged to its own association.[3] Like Beddome, Turner was given an honorary M.A. from the Baptist College in Providence, Rhode Island. Unlike Beddome, Turner was the author of many volumes, including one promoting open communion.[4] We know that he was a friend and correspondent of the Congregationalist author Isaac Watts (1674–1748) and of Baptist ministers such as Robert Robinson (1735–1790) and John Rippon (1751–1836).

Bourton is just over 30 miles west of Abingdon and from 1774 a summertime double lecture series began in the two churches along with others nearby. Otherwise there are no obvious links between Beddome and Turner beyond their being contemporaries and fellow Baptist ministers, which Turner admits in his letter. However, in 1762 the long letter below was written out of great concern for Beddome. There is nothing extant in the known life of Beddome that would confirm the view that Turner takes of his state that, at the age of 45, he was suffering from "a nervous disorder, attended with spiritual darkness and distress." The only hint we have is the way that Thomas Brooks, in a history of the Bourton church that was written in 1861, describes the years 1759–1763 as

---

[2] Turner is under-represented biographically, as there is no proper study of this significant Baptist hymn writer, pastor, and theologian. A blue plaque exists on the house next to Abingdon Baptist Church where he lived (35 Ock Street, Abingdon). It reads "Daniel Turner 1710-1798 Baptist Minister Theologian Hymn Writer lived here 1748-1798."

[3] The Abingdon Association was founded in 1652 and the Midland Association in 1655.

[4] The pamphlet in favour of open communion, *A Modest Plea for Free Communion at the Lord's Table; Particularly between the Baptists and the Paedobaptists*, was published anonymously in 1772 under the pseudonym *Candidus*. It was almost identical to one by Bourton-born pastor John Colett Ryland (1723–1792) with the pseudonym *Pacificus*. Interestingly, another work by Turner was a volume of *Letters religious and moral* which appeared in 1766 (2nd ed., 1793). Other works include *An Introduction to Psalmody* (1737); *An Abstract of English Grammar and Rhetoric* (London, 1739); *Divine Songs, Hymns, and other Poems* (Reading, 1747); *A Compendium of Social Religion* (1758; 2nd ed., Bristol, 1778); *Short Meditations on Select Portions of Scripture* (Abingdon, 1771; 3rd ed. 1803); *Charity the Bond of Perfection. A sermon* (Abingdon, 1780); *Devotional Poetry vindicated against Dr Johnson* (Oxford, 1785); *Essays on Important Subjects* (Oxford, 1787); *Poems Devotional and Moral* (privately printed, 1794); *Common Sense, or the Plain Man's Answer to the Question, Whether Christianity be a Religion worthy of our choice?* (1797).

"the period of depression that had now set in" before a good harvest in 1764.[5]

The Letter[6]
[Introduction]
You may possibly think it strange, my good brother, that I who have so little personal acquaintance with you, and know so little particularly, of your case, should give you the trouble of so long a letter, as the enclosed—and I confess it a liberty I am not sufficiently warranted to take. Nevertheless, I having myself once felt so much from a situation not perhaps much unlike yours, I was, more than I should else have been, affected with the short hints of your case in your last favour with the association Letter,[7] that I could not easily resist the inclination I found in my mind, to say something that might administer to your comfort through the Divine blessing, though I confess I had no thought when I set out of going half this length. If I have been impertinent, I did not design to be so, and the rectitude of my intention, and your goodness, I trust, will plead my excuse. I am however, wishing to see you.
Yours sincerely,
D Turner
Abingdon, [Saturday] Sep 4 1762

[The ode]
The Ode on the other side I composed for the comfort of a friend in distress, as well as to give vent to my own thoughts upon the subject. It proved a means of her refreshment and pleasure, it may possibly answer the like end with you, please therefore to accept of it as an instance of my good intention.

---

[5] Thomas Brooks, *Pictures of the Past: The History of the Baptist Church, Bourton-on-the-Water* (London: Judd & Glass, 1861), 50.

[6] The letter has been divided into parts for ease of reading.

[7] One minister in an Association would be appointed to write what was known as the "Association Letter" each year, what one circular letter optimistically called "a body of divinity in miniature" (*The Beauty of Social Religion; Or, the Nature and Glory of a Gospel Church, Represented in a Circular Letter from the Baptist ministers and Messengers, Assembled at Oakham, in Rutlandshire, May 20, 21, 1777* [Northampton, 1777], 2). This circular letter was printed on behalf of the churches. Beddome wrote the Midland Association Letter in 1759 (the first time it was done in this way) and in 1765 (*The Circular Letter from the Elders and Messengers of the Several Baptist Churches, Meeting at Aulcester, Bengeworth, Birmingham, Bourton, Bromsgrove, Bridgnorth, Bewdley, Hooknorton, Leominster, Middleton, Pershore, Sutton, Tewkesbury, Upton, Warwick, [having also received Letters from Dudley, Leicester, and Worcester,] met in Association at Bourton on the Water, the 14th and 15th of August, 1765, and maintaining the Doctrines of Free Grace, in opposition to Arminianism and Socinianism: and the Necessity of good Works in opposition to Libertinism and real Antinomianism* [Worcester, 1765]). The reference here is more likely to be to the letter each church in an association would send by way of report. Beddome appears to have done Turner the courtesy of sending him the Bourton letter sent to the Midland Association in 1762.

1. Jesus, full of all compassion, Hear thy humble suppliant's cry;
Let me know thy great salvation: See I languish, faint, and die.
2. Guilty, but with heart relenting Overwhelm'd with helpless grief,
Prostrate at thy feet repenting, Send, O send me quick relief!
3. Whither should a wretch be flying, But to him who comfort gives?—
Whither, from the dread of dying, But to him who ever lives
4. While I view thee, wounded, grieving, Breathless on the cursed tree,
Fain I'd feel my heart believing That thou sufferedst thus for me
5. With thy righteousness and Spirit, I am more than angels blest;
Heir with thee, all things inherit,—Peace, and joy, and endless rest.
6. Without thee, the world possessing, I should be a wretch undone,
Search through heaven, the land of blessing Seeking good and finding none
7. Hear then, blessed Saviour, hear me; My soul cleaveth to the dust;
Send the Comforter to cheer me; Lo I in thee I put my trust.
8. On the word thy blood hath sealed Hangs my everlasting all:
Let thy arm be now revealed: Stay, O stay me, lest I fall!
9. In the world of endless ruin. Let it never. Lord, be said,
Here's a soul that perish'd, suing For the boasted Saviour's aid.
10. Saved—the deed shall spread new glory Through the shining realms above!
Angels sing the pleasing story, All enraptured with thy love.[8]

[The main body of the letter]
Dear Brother,
I do pity you with all my heart, and that not barely from a principle of common benevolence, or even Christian charity, but from real experience of perhaps the like, or worse condition myself. Yours, I suppose to be a nervous disorder, attended with spiritual darkness and distress; if so, by attending to my story, and the reflections arising from it, you may possibly find some consolation.

[Turner's experience 1744/5]
About eighteen years ago, I fell into a deep and dreadful oppression of spirits, the very remembrance of which is ready to make me shudder, even to this day.[9]

---

[8] This became one of Turner's best-known hymns. It is one of four of Turner's hymns collected in John Ash (1724–1779) and Caleb Evans' (1737–1791) *A Collection of Hymns Adapted to Public* Worship, 3rd ed. (1769, Bristol, 1778), 221–223, as well as in John Rippon's (1751–1836), *A Selection of Hymns from the Best Authors, Intended to be an Appendix to Dr Watts's Psalms and Hymns* (London, 1787), hymn 295.

[9] Turner pastored in Reading from 1743 to 1748. September 1744 was the time of the death of his first wife, Ann Fanch, sister of James Fanch (1704–1767), who was the pastor at Romsey. He may be alluding to this although it sounds rather as though he himself was unwell. Turner later remarried a Reading woman, a Mrs Lucas. With Ann, he had two sons who did not survive him. There were no children with Mrs Lucas.

There was some great disorder of body, but my mind was still more disordered, and felt the weight of all. Every thing of a distressing and terrifying nature, as to my spiritual concerns, especially, seemed to be present with me. I thought myself the most miserable being this side hell. Often wondered to see people afflict themselves about the common calamities of life. They appeared mere trifles, Infirmities that might be easily borne; but mine was a Wounded Spirit,[10] torn with the clearest apprehensions of the malignancy of sin, and the displeasure of an Almighty God. I not only could not see any interest I had in his pardoning mercy, but feared I was given up by him to the Tyranny of my corruptions, so that I should certainly fall into some gross and scandalous sin, as a just judgment upon me, and so be left to perish with the most aggravated guilt, a monument of the Divine resentment against false pretenders of religion. I often wished to die even though I could but dread the consequence.

I sought the Lord by prayer and the other means of grace,[11] day and night, but he still hid his face from me, now and then a glimpse of hope would break in upon me, but it was of short continuance. The Bible seemed as a sealed book in which I could meet with no comfort, though often much to aggravate my distress and increase my terrors. I endeavoured to examine myself, and search for the evidences of renewing grace in my heart,[12] but all in vain, the more I searched, the more dark and confounded and distressed I grew. I continued to preach indeed to others, but very often with this heart-sinking conclusion, that I myself was a castaway. Sometimes even in the midst of my work, the melancholy darkness would rush in upon my soul so that I was ready to sink down in the pulpit. Though for the most part I was tolerable during the exercise, yet I generally went to the pulpit and returned from it with trembling heart and knees. Many passages in the book of Job, and the Psalms, particularly the 88th Psalm, I felt as I read them, with peculiar sensations. Thus I continued for more than twelve months, enjoying scarcely two comfortable days together.[13]

---

[10] This is an allusion to Proverbs 18:14, "The spirit of a man will sustain his infirmity; but a wounded spirit who can bear?" Modern translations refer to a broken or crushed spirit.

[11] By this he, of course, means the Word read and preached and the Lord's Supper and perhaps reading and fellowship.

[12] Turner refers to "the evidences of grace" six times in the letter. This refers to the practice of looking at one's own life for evidence of God's grace in order to obtain assurance. It is the sort of thing encouraged by William Guthrie (1620–1665) in *The Christian's Great Interest* (c. 1658) or Jonathan Edwards (1703–1758) in his *Religious Affections* (1746). Turner appears to be slightly skeptical of this approach saying that in dark periods it is perhaps better not to look for such evidences. At one point he says, "I found I had unawares laid too great a stress upon evidences of grace, and looked too much to them for my comfort, and too little to Christ."

[13] Psalm 88 is the psalm that bleakly ends "Lover and friend hast thou put far from me, and mine acquaintance into darkness." John Gill (1697–1771) calls it "a sorrowful and mournful song" (John Gill, *An*

At length I came to this resolution, (viz.) to give up the point of proving myself a child of God already (which was what I had been labouring at all along) as a necessary medium of my comfort, and grant that I was a vile, sinful, and every way unworthy creature, admit the whole charge brought against me, and seek my remedy in Christ. For I argued, there was forgiveness with God for the chief of sinners.[14]

[His exhortation]
The Blood of Christ could cleanse from All sin—and therefore from mine—He came to call not the Righteous, but Sinners to repentance; sinners without distinction of degrees, sinners as such, and because they were such. 'Twas said that Whosoever would, might come and take of the waters of life freely, and that he would in no wise cast them out.[15] Hence I was led to observe that if I could not go to him as a Saint, I might go as a Sinner. I resolved therefore to lay aside my enquiries after the evidence of my interest in him as one of his renewed people, and look entirely to him from whom all renewing grace, and the evidences of it, must come, look to him as a guilty, polluted, perishing creature, that had no hope, no succour, but in the pure Mercy of God through him. And thus I was led to such views of the all-sufficiency of the great Redeemer, and his willingness to save even the worst of sinners, such as I could best conclude myself to be, as silenced all my doubts, scattered my fears, and gave the most delightful peace and joy to my conscience. I now learnt indeed what I thought I had (and perhaps really had) learnt before, (viz.) To live by Faith alone upon the Son of God;[16] to make his sacrifice and righteousness my constant refuge, and draw all my consolations thence.

I found I had unawares laid too great a stress upon evidences of grace, and looked too much to them for my comfort, and too little to Christ. I plainly saw that with all the brightest evidences of grace about me, I was still a sinner, and must apply my Saviour as such, in order to give life and vigour to my consolations and hopes: and that the spiritual life in me must be perpetually supplied from the same fountain from whence I had derived what I had already experienced. I found that the seasons of Darkness were not the proper seasons for seeking after evidences; but that the immediate and leading duty was, trusting in the Name of the Lord. I saw more clearly than ever that in the great business of acceptance with God, I could bring no righteousness of my

---

Exposition of the Old Testament, in which are recorded the Original of Mankind, of the Several Nations of the World, and of the Jewish National in particular [London, 1765], 4:71).

[14] 1 Timothy 1:15.

[15] Allusions here are to 1 John 1:7 and Luke 5:32, and parallel verses are Revelation 22:17 and John 6:37.

[16] Romans 1:17; Galatians 3:11; Hebrews 10:38. All depend on Habakkuk 2:4.

own, that would avail; but that as a creature utterly undone myself, I must look to him who takes away the sin of the world. That God never rejected any, that seriously and in earnest applied to him, because they were more guilty and unworthy than others, or accepted others because they were less so; and in a word, that as the best must so the worst may come to him, through a penitent faith in the precious blood and righteousness of his Son, with equal assurance of a gracious welcome. And from that time to this (I bless God for his great mercy) I have never had any long continued doubt of my interest in his saving love. Whenever darkness and distress assault me, I am enabled to look to him who is the light and consolation of Israel;[17] and remember that his grace is as free to me as another, and that he is as willing as able to save to the uttermost, All that come unto God by him. I send you this account, my dear brother, thus circumstantially, to let you see, if possible, that there has no uncommon temptation overtaken you.[18]

Remember though you may walk in darkness and have No light, yet there is a gracious provision made for all such in the Gospel,[19] in the very nature and constitution of it in general, as well as in its precious promises and declarations in particular; so that if we take this Gospel just as it lies in. our Bibles, we shall see that there is not the least room for even the worst of sinners to despair. For even to the impenitent and unbelieving the Gospel opens a remote hope, as it is the means of leading them to repentance and producing faith: and to the awakened and sensible sinner, an immediate hope, as the means of that holiness and comfort he seeks. The Grace that saves must be entirely, absolutely free to Them; or else in the just and full conviction of their sin and guilt, it would be impossible any of them could have hope.

You want to see more of the image of God in you, more of the saint and less of the sinner; the desire is right and good; but remember, were you the purest saint on earth, that purity, though an occasion, would not be the primary ground and reason of your comfort. We are begotten again to a lively hope, not by even our evangelical holiness, but by the Resurrection of Christ from the dead,[20] and the facts, doctrines, and promises connected with it, credited and trusted as they lie in the Bible. The greatest saint must depend upon the same righteousness and strength in Christ as the greatest sinner; and the latter is as welcome to that dependence as the former; if, having the comfort of that dependence, he makes it his serious care to purify himself from all filthiness of

---

[17] Luke 2:25, 32.

[18] 1 Corinthians 10:13.

[19] Isaiah 50:10.

[20] 1 Peter 1:3.

flesh and spirit, perfecting holiness in the fear of God.[21] Though we are never so poor, and miserable and blind and naked, yet we may apply to Christ, even in this miserable condition, with assurance of success, as appears from his own word, if we apply with a view to our deliverance from the power as well as the guilt of our sins.[22]

[The danger of self-righteousness]
All this you very well know, and therefore need none of my instructions; but I meant not to instruct, but to stir up your mind by way of remembrance.[23]

I scarce ever knew a disconsolate Christian, however notionally clear, in the doctrine of the gospel and the way of a sinner's acceptance with God, but that as to fact and the real exercise of his mind, was some how entangled in his own righteousness; and built his comforts and hopes so much upon his evidences of renewing grace, as in some culpable degree to overlook the only Name given under heaven[24] for our consolation, and so far as to miss his aim and disappoint his desires and expectations. Terrified with the charge of guilt, his first attempt usually is, to prove himself not guilty, or at least to extenuate it, and prove it consistent with a state of grace, this diverts his attention from the proper object in that case, and to, which he should first look, viz. the great atonement and everlasting righteousness of Jesus; for under all convictions of sin, the proper question with respect to our comfort is, not how guilty we are, but how we may find forgiveness? And the answer is through a penitent faith in that atonement and righteousness; for be the guilt less or more, this only can purge the conscience from it, and give us the peace of God;[25] and for this it is all-sufficient: or take it thus.

We are sinners—we hear of a Saviour, and what he has done, and suffered, and is doing for our salvation—the questions are—

1. Are these things so? Are the facts and doctrines, declarations and promises of the Gospel true? If we have any doubt here, our business is with the evidences of the Divinity of the Gospel.

2. Are those declarations and promises, etc. free and open to All without exception, who see their need of the Grace therein implied?

If we have any doubt here, the due consideration of the nature and design

---

[21] 2 Corinthians 7:1.

[22] Revelation 3:17.

[23] 2 Peter 3:1.

[24] Acts 4:12.

[25] Hebrews 9:14; Philippians 4:7.

of the gospel—the infinite worth of the atonement[26]—the stile and language of the invitations and promises, etc., will afford abundant means of satisfaction—Nothing in the world can be more true and certain, than, that God so loved the World as to send his only begotten Son into it; and 'tis as true, that whosoever believeth on him shall not perish, but have everlasting life.[27] Which believing is neither more nor less, as to what is essential to the point, than an hearty and sincere crediting of the truth of this declaration; and an humble penitent reliance upon the promise connected with it, as the Word of the eternal God, from a sense of the need of his grace, and with a view to the obtaining it. It is as our Lord himself represents it in the context, just the same thing, as the stung Israelites looking to the brazen serpent for a cure.[28] Though wounded ever so deeply, if they cast an eye upon this medium, with a faith in the divine appointment and promises, they were as assuredly healed, as if they had received only the slightest injury; and that this was the case of all who so looked, without exception.

Under convictions of our lost condition, and desire after deliverance, the first thing is believing, or looking by faith to Jesus, and trusting in his atonement, righteousness and power. This is the foundation of all prayer, and every approach to God. For he that cometh unto God must believe that he is, and that he is a rewarder of all that diligently seek him, etc.;[29] He that would find light, and life and peace with God, must first believe there are such blessings, and the way in which they are to be obtained, viz. through Jesus Christ. Without some sort of credit to the divine testimony, some trust in the divine promises, it would be impossible to have any real hope towards God, and without hope there can be nothing done in religion. Instead therefore of these enquiries and reasonings about matters not immediately pertaining to the exercise of faith, our business is to apply ourselves directly to that exercise, assuring ourselves of the truth of the promises, and relying upon them in humble confidence that they shall be made good to us.

But here perhaps the distressed Christian may be ready to say, "Faith is the gift of God,[30] and I don't find he has given me that gift, I cannot believe, though I much desire it." To such a one I would answer, Faith is undoubtedly the gift of God, but the power to believe and trust, does not lie where such as you generally think it does, viz. in a certain active energy in the mind, but in the

---

[26] This Calvinist understanding can be traced back at least as far as Anselm (d. 1109).

[27] John 3:16.

[28] John 3:14, 15; Numbers 21:7–9.

[29] Hebrews 11:6.

[30] Ephesians 2:8.

fullness and clearness of the evidence of the Truth and a capacity to receive it, for all faith begins in persuasion, and persuasion is the result of evidence. Hence we read of believers being persuaded of the promises,[31] and that faith is the evidence (conviction or evincement) of things not seen.[32] We cannot doubt of the testimony of God when once we are convinced it is his testimony; nor, if sensible of our misery and really desirous of deliverance, can we avoid putting a confidence in those promises of deliverance that we believe God has made us. These acts of the mind will follow in the circumstances supposed unless we purposely and wilfully withhold them against conviction, which no serious mind can do. Our inability to believe, therefore, lies rather in the want of light than of power, i.e. the want of evidence as to the truth, reality, and importance of the object of our faith, or the want of a capacity to perceive it. Both these are the gifts of God. The means of both he has put into our hands, with assurances of blessing the Use of them. Faith cometh by hearing and hearing by the word of God.[33] Upon that word, the marks of Divinity and truth are imprinted with the most glorious and affecting evidence.

The glorious Spirit that dictated it, still breathes in it. It is spirit and life, the power of God to salvation.[34] It enlightens the soul, it convinces of sin and of righteousness,[35] and thus tends to produce in us a just sense of our misery and the suitableness, excellency, and all-sufficiency of Christ as a Saviour. A serious and attentive regard to this word, accompanied with prayer, and that degree of faith such a conduct implies as already given, must be the sure way of increasing faith, and filling the mind with true consolation. Hear and your soul shall live.[36]

[Doubt]

But there is perhaps still a difficulty that the humble Christian cannot easily get over. He doubts his right to the promises of Grace, but here also he generally mistakes. He lays it upon some unattained qualification in himself, and which he thinks he must attain before he can embrace the promise in question, and which he seeks not by faith in Christ, but by some work or works of the law, some duties, which not being done in faith, can avail nothing;[37] and thus, as

---

[31] Hebrews 11:13; Romans 4:21.

[32] Hebrews 11:1.

[33] Romans 10:17.

[34] Romans 1:16.

[35] John 16:8.

[36] Isaiah 55:3.

[37] Galatians 5:6.

the prophet expresses it, he spends his money for that which is not bread, and, labour for that which satisfieth not.[38]

The primary ground of all right that sinful creatures can have in the gospel mercy, is, the free and express grant of it from God himself. The primary medium of putting us into possession of that right is the atonement and righteousness of Christ; the next is that of believing the Testimony of God concerning these things and trusting in it. This is the scriptural representation. The qualifications which the perplexed and disconsolate Christian seeks with so much anxiety, therefore, are rather the effects and consequence of this grant, atonement and faith, and not preliminaries to believing, or preparatories to faith. It is true, there must, in the nature of the things, be some sense of the evil of sin and desire of deliverance, without which little regard will be paid to the Gospel Mercy and way; but these his very uneasiness and distress shew that he has already; and by the very terms of the promise, he that is weary and heavy laden may trust in Christ for rest. If he thirst for them he may come and take of the waters of life freely.[39] And indeed what qualifications can a guilty, polluted, impotent creature bring to his Saviour, beyond a sight and feeling of his misery and a desire of deliverance Holiness in principle, and the fruits of it in practice, are necessary to the final enjoyment of eternal life; but not necessary to our believing the Gospel promises; because that belief itself is necessary to our holiness; for the heart said to be purified by faith. The proper answer to every one that says what shall I do to be saved? is that of the apostle, Believe on the Lord Jesus Christ.[40] Believe what God has testified concerning his Son, as the great propitiation for sin, and you will find that the experience of the efficacy of his blood, to purge the conscience from dead works,[41] and of his power to save us from our spiritual blindness and depravity, and every evil, will follow. It is for want of entering thoroughly into this distinction, and mistaking the nature of faith, and the order and place appointed for it, in the great affair of salvation, that so many sincere Christians live so great strangers to the solid and lasting consolations of Christ.

[Conclusion]
Forgive me, my dear friend and brother, that I have run on this tiresome length: I don't however mean to teach you, of whom I am better qualified to learn, but to remind you of such things as have a tendency to disperse the gloom that may hang over your mind. However, be of good courage and wait on the Lord, and

---

[38] Isaiah 55:2.

[39] Matthew 11:28–30; Revelation 22:17.

[40] A reference to Acts 16:30, preceded by an allusion to Acts 15:9.

[41] Hebrews 9:14.

your strength in his due time shall be renewed. He is pleased with those who hope in his mercy; hope therefore in him, and you will yet praise his delivering grace.[42]

Let me have your prayers, and believe me your sincere Friend and affectionate Brother in Christ.

D Turner

---

[42] See Psalm 27:14 and Psalm 147:11 with an allusion to Psalm 42:5 and Psalm 43:5.

An uncatalogued baptism-sermon by Joseph Kinghorn (1766–1832)

Edited by Baiyu Andrew Song

Baiyu Andrew Song is the Research Associate and Teaching Fellow at the Andrew Fuller Centre for Baptist Studies at Heritage College and Seminary, Cambridge, Ontario.

Introduction
Perhaps no one described an eighteenth-century public baptism service better than the celebrated Robert Robinson (1735–1790). In his lengthy treatise, *The History of Baptism*, Robinson reported that Andrew Gifford, Jr. (1700–1784) preached a sermon explaining the sacrament upon a moveable pulpit, read a hymn, and prayed, before he went down into the water to baptize forty-eight candidates at Whittlesford, Cambridgeshire.[1] A year later, in a cold, dark, foggy spring dawn, Joseph Kinghorn baptised a family of five in the River Bure just outside of Aylsham, Norfolk.[2] For months, Kinghorn rode twelve miles from Norwich north to the market town Aylsham to preach. With the fear of persecution, Kinghorn performed baptism first, and afterwards, they returned to the house where he lodged and changed their clothes, the young pastor "addressed them on the serious nature of the profession they had made &c & after joining in Prayer again they were left me & went on their way rejoicing."[3]

---

[1] Robert Robinson, *The History of Baptism* (London, 1790), 541–542.

[2] Joseph Kinghorn to David and Elizabeth Kinghorn, May 9, 1791, D/KIN 2/1791 no. 659, Kinghorn Papers (Angus Library and Archive, Regent's Park College, Oxford), 1–2.

[3] Joseph Kinghorn to David and Elizabeth Kinghorn, May 9, 1791, D/KIN 2/1791 no. 659, Kinghorn

How did Kinghorn address his new converts? We do not know. Nevertheless, Kinghorn understood the value of preaching sermons on baptism, as he explained to his father in 1792:

> Tis a subject so circumscribed that one is ready to suppose 2 or 3 sermons would exhaust it yet I know not how something fresh always states up. In thinking upon it I was very much struck with the thought that if it was possible to set aside the Evidence of adult Bap^m. (especially the mode) the evidence of every part of the New Testament might be set aside in the same way.[4]

Curiously, though Particular Baptists during the Hanoverian dynasty antagonistically defended their conviction of credobaptism by immersion, they had rarely published sermons preached at baptism services.[5] It is, therefore, significant to discover this uncatalogued sermon manuscript in the Kinghorn Papers at Angus Library and Archive, which was prepared a few months before Kinghorn's sudden death and preached at a baptism service.

According to the library's catalogue (September 1999), the folder that was marked as "Kinghorn Letters D/KIN 2/1832" contains

---

Papers (Angus Library and Archive, Regent's Park College, Oxford), 1.

[4] Joseph Kinghorn to David and Elizabeth Kinghorn, April 2, 1792, D/KIN 2/1792 no. 714, Kinghorn Papers (Angus Library and Archive, Regent's Park College, Oxford), 1.

[5] One exception is John Gill's (1697–1771) sermon (Gill, *Baptism a Divine Commandment to be Observed. Being a Sermon Preached at Barbican, Octob. 9, 1765. At the Baptism of the Reverend Mr. Robert Carmichael, Minister of the Gospel in Edinburgh* [London, 1765]), which was preached at the baptism of Robert Carmichael (d. 1774), a Scottish Anti-burgher Seceder minister who became a Baptist after reading John Glas' (1695–1773) *Testimony to the King of Martyrs Concerning His Kingdom* (1729) in the 1750s. Carmichael came to London and was baptised by Gill on October 9, 1765. Later with Archibald McLean (1733–1812), Carmichael established the first Baptist chapel in Scotland. See Robert W. Oliver, "John Gill (1697–1771): His Life and Ministry," in *The Life and Thought of John Gill (1697–1771): An Tercentennial Appreciation*, edited by Michael A.G. Haykin (Leiden, the Netherlands; New York; Köln, Germany: Brill, 1997), 36; Nathan Finn, ed., *Apologetic Works 5: Strictures on Sandemanianism*, The Complete Works of Andrew Fuller, Volume 9 (Berlin; Boston, MA: De Gruyter, 2016), 13–14; Brian R. Talbot, *The Search for a Common Identity: The Origins of the Baptist Union of Scotland 1800–1870* (Milton Keynes, Buckinghamshire: Paternoster, 2003), 29–30.

Another example is a sermon on Acts 8:36–38 by John Brown (d. 1800) of Kettering (Brown, *A Sermon Preached at a Public Administration of Baptism; Interspersed and enlarged with Testimonies from Learned and Judicious Writers, Who Espoused Infant-Sprinkling. To which is added, Hymns sung on that Solemn Occasion* [London, 1764]). This work was so popular that within a year, four editions were printed for sale. Also see Timothy D. Whelan, ed., *Baptist Autographs in the John Rylands University Library of Manchester, 1741–1845* (Macon, GA: Mercer University Press, 2009), 360; Robert W. Oliver, *History of the English Calvinistic Baptists 1771–1892: From John Gill to C.H. Spurgeon* (Edinburgh: Banner of Truth Trust, 2006), 66–70.

letters incl. Joseph Jarrom of Wisbeach to JK, seeking advice on Crooke Place church (10 Feb); letter from R. S. Foster of Dublin to messrs Wilkin & Co., booksellers of Norwich, concerning JK's death and asking if he could buy a memento from JK's library (18 Sp); letter from WMB to Miss priest quoting utterances by JK (17 Oct.); note copied from the flyleaf of cousin Norton's diary for 1833 referring to the last days of JK in 1832, and with later notes to 1854.

Within this folder, there are six items in total, and the last item is a folded manuscript written in four folios. By a closer examination, they are two sermon manuscripts, written probably by Kinghorn. The first sermon is one and a half pages in length, and it was preached on August 22, 1832, on Jeremiah 35:14–15. The second sermon is six pages in length, and it was preached on May 2, 1832, on Colossians 2:12. Specifically, the author indicated that the second sermon was preached "at the Baptism of Mr. Hanner Ann Hanner and William Norton Jr."[6] Calligraphically, the texts are profoundly identical to Kinghorn's earlier letters, and the only exception is the consistent omission of the tittle and arm in letters "i" and "t," as well as the usage of Greek epsilon instead of an "e" in English. Nevertheless, Kinghorn's biographer Martin Hood Wilkin (1832–1904) provided a significant clue regarding these manuscripts' authorship. On August 19, 1832, then 66-year-old Kinghorn unknowingly preached his last Sunday sermon on 2 Peter 1:7. On Wednesday, August 23, 1832, Kinghorn delivered an evening lecture at St. Mary's chapel, with which "his public labours closed, on which occasion he selected the remarkable account of the Rechabites in the 35th of Jeremiah. It was an interesting and striking address."[7] Thus, the first text in this article is a manuscript of Kinghorn's last lecture or sermon. As both texts were written by the same hand, it is prudent to argue that we have discovered two uncatalogued sermons by Kinghorn soon before his decease.

Notes on the Texts

The following two texts are transcribed according to their original presentation, without any additions. Unless it is indicated with square brackets, all parts are original. Unlike the first text, Kinghorn did not write anything in the margins of the second text, except seven "q"-like shorthand letters. The other place

---

[6] Joseph Kinghorn, unnumbered sermon manuscripts, D/KIN 2/1832, Kinghorn Papers (Angus Library and Archive, Regent's Park College, Oxford), 3.

[7] It is noticed that Wilken was confused with the date, as he mistakenly wrote "With the Wednesday evening lecture on the 23rd of August." Wilkin's date was a Thursday, instead of a Wednesday. Martin Hood Wilkin, *Joseph Kinghorn, of Norwich* (Norwich: Fletcher and Alexander; London: Arthur Hall, 1855), in *The Life and Work of Joseph Kinghorn*, edited by Terry Wolever (Springfield, MO: Particular Baptist Press, 1995), 1:455.

where Kinghorn used shorthand letters is in the nota bene: one letter with the shape of "V" with an arm and the other looks like the Hebrew letter kaf. In the manuscript, the nota bene is crossed out by two vertical lines drew with ink.

Text I
Jeremiah 35 v. 14, 15   Augt. 22d 1832.   [1]
The Rechabites and the Appeal of the Lord to Israel
taken from them.

The Rechabites were of the family of the Kenites *{death of   }   [5]
                                                 {descendent from}
Moses Father in Law who dwell in the Land of Canaan
on the enhance of the People into that Land and enjoyed its
general privileges but in the Strict sense of the words were
never the People of Israel   [10]
　　For some reason now unknown their Father
enjoined upon them not to drink wine and his posterity
obeyed the command he also directed them to dwell in
tentssee vv. 6–10.
　　Neither the Lord nor the Prophet made any observat^n. [15]
upon the necessity of this request but the Lord took it at the
foundation of appeal and sent his prophet to make it.
　　　　　　　　　　　　　　　　(v. 13:
　　And in the result we find God promised to this
people the consumed existence which a late traveller
hasd *justified by stating that he met with a party of   [20]
People who said they were of that family. as if the
conscientious regard to precepts which were not of Divine
authority when there was nothing in them contract to the
word of God was in his view the mark of that state of
mind upon which he looked with favor and shewed   [25]
a cultivated subdued spirit which would and could attend
to better things
　　And now saith the Lord of these Rechabites obeyed
their Father with conscientious attention will you not
look at them and receive instruction. How much more   [30]
should you have attended to me. I have sent you Prophets
from time to time with suitable admonitions yet you
attended not to them How far is your conduct below
that of the Rechabites!
Obs. I. The Israelites were distinguished by the means   [35]

afforded than for the purpose of keeping them to the
acknowledgement of the only true God.
    By his word—Appointments—*<u>Misery</u>—providence
               cases
and as many ~~consequences~~ by his grace in their heart; Still
more by occasional admonitions. In addition to all these   [40]
by his prophets: and all this by Evident and direct authority
appealing to them.

[Page 2]
Obs. II Yet still they rebelled and harkened not unto   [1]
him: their reason might have told them that they
*passions were wrong but their {*positions } ([?].) led them astray; their
               {possessions}
connections with heathens entrusted them; their ambition
their political situation; all these had their influence. and   [5]
hence they were threatened with the punishment which
the Lord had told them should come. v. 17.
    <u>1.</u> When God gives means [?] mercy. But men are
apt to despise them: they may attend to the form when
they do no more. they may and often do neglect these   [10]
*<u>draws</u> whenever a temptation *{drives } them aside these things
               {throws}
will come to * <u>view (?)</u> beforye God and they will be allowed
with their effects read Rev^{ns}.. c. 2&3.
    <u>2.</u> When God begins to fulfil his threatenings
men should fear before him. The Jews had time for   [15]
reflection in Babylon and before they came that:
<u>then</u> they recollected what they had lost Ps: 137. Dan: 9
    3. 'Tis a great blessing when the Judgments
of God lead men to repentance for they are then not
given in rain even respecting their present effect   [20]

Text II
Col: II. 12.   May 2d. 1832   [1]
    at the Baptism of Mr. Hanner Ann Hanner and
            William Norton Jr.[8]

---

[8] William Norton, Jr. (1812–1890) was born on December 24, 1812 to William and Mary Culley (1781–1821) Norton, members of Aylsham Baptist Chapel. According to the church's register, Joseph Kinghorn was the presenting office to register the junior's birth (The National Archives of the UK, *General Register Office: Registers of Births, Marriages and Deaths Surrendered to the Non-Parochial Registers Commissions of 1837*

Buried with him----from the dead. [5]

In the passage here before us the apostles great
object is to shew the sufficiency of Christ for all we want
and the connection existing between him and those
that belong or bind and this he illustrates by the instruction [10]
of Baptism pointing out that they were dead with Christ
buried with him, are risen with him and quickened by
him and after stating the consequences of this sentiment
in the remaining part of the chapter in the next he
pursues it still further. [15]
From the mention in the preceding verse of Christians made
being circumcised with the circumcision^without hands. an
opinion is currently urged that here is Evidence that
Baptism is the Christian circumcision and that the
institution appointed by the Lord came in the place of [20]
that which had belonged to the Jewish ceremony[9]
Surely no argument was ever more inconclusive
particularly when it is intended to make way for the

---

and 1857, Class Number RG 4, Piece Number 361, Norwich, St Margarets Chapel (Baptist), 1761–1822, [56]). William Senior "built Baptist chapels at Old Buckenham and Attleborough, Norfolk" (Geoffrey Ralph Breed, "Norton, William," in *Dictionary of Evangelical Biography 1730–1860*, edited by Donald M. Lewis [Peabody, MA: Hendrickson, 2004], 2:833). After his baptism, Norton, Jr. went and studied at Stepney Academy from 1833 to 1836. Though he applied to become a missionary in the East Indies, the Baptist Missionary Society rejected Norton's application due to his poor health. From 1826 to 1840, Norton then succeeded William Newman (1773–1835) and ministered the congregation at Bow Street in east London. From 1838 to 1840, Norton served as an editor of *The Primitive Communionist* magazine, and later an editor of *The Primitive Church Magazine* (1841–1847). Due to health issues, Norton and his wife Mary Ann Franks moved constantly since 1847 and finally settled down at Chulmleigh, Devon, where he died on August 12, 1890. As a scholar, Norton translated the New Testament into Spanlish, and most of the Peshitta New Testament into English. Norton also compiled *Hymns of Hope, founded on the Psalms and the New Covenant* (London: Elliot Stock, 1879). Along with George Pritchard (1773–1852), and Robert Overbury (1812–1868), Norton was instrumental to form the Baptist Tract Society, and to promote the principles of strict communion (see Geoffrey Ralph Breed, *Particular Baptists in Victorian England and their Strict Communion Organizations* [Broadway, Didcot: Baptist Historical Society, 2003], 30–70, 71–141). Significantly, when Kinghorn's congregation was split over the terms of communion under the pastorate of George Gould (1818–1882), Norton actively participated in the debate and edited *Baptist Chapel, St Mary's, Norwich. The Suit—Attorney-General versus Gould and Others, in the Rolls Court: Its Origin, the Proceedings, Pleadings, and Judgment* (London: J. Briscoe; Houlston and Wright, 1860).

[9] See Joseph Kinghorn, *A Defence of Infant Baptist, its best Confutation: Being a Reply to Mr. Peter Edwards' Candid Reasons for Renouncing the Principles of Anti-paedo-baptism, on His Own Ground* (Norwich, 1795).

Baptism of Infants Observe the apostles language; you are
circumcised with the circumcision made <u>without hands</u> [25]
in putting off (the)? <u>body of the sins of the flesh</u> by the circumcise
of Christ: it is the circumcision, ~~not of the~~ not of an
external kind but inward of the heart and was not in
the external operation but in putting away the body of the
flesh. and not having (?) that body to rule over us: this [30]
does apply to the <u>regenerated</u> Christian: it does not to the
infant; nor can it apply: and it is these who are of this
<u>regenerated</u> description that the apostle applies to and <u>says</u> (?)
"you are buried with me in Baptism &c"

    When we had lately occasion to call your [35]
attention to the institution of Baptism we then noticed
the objects the qualifications (?) the authority, the
example of the Lord and the character of the
institution as the answer of a good conscience towards
God. But we now take a view of the subject that is [40]
different from what ha~~ds~~ for some time engaged us
and which relates

    I. To the mode of Baptism has referred to and
    II. To the view given of the connection between the
    believer and his Lord here pointed out [45]

[p. 4 of the folios]
I. The first is the mode to which here is a [1]
<u>direct allusion</u> made "<u>Buried</u> with Christ in Baptism"

    From all* observation I believe that all great
objection to our views of the subject at large arises from
our supporting the mode that was of old appointed [5]
from
~~the~~^observations which we hear at different times
this is pretty evident at times it has bear (,—by those
(who are?) convinced that we are right but for some reasons are
not acting with us,—) <u>acknowledged</u> in plain terms

    But then if the mode we support be that of [10]
the word of God <u>whose blame is it? is it ours?</u> Or if we
only are doing what the Lord appointed <u>is it his blame?</u>
If he in appointing Baptism meant it to be immersion, by
the words he used & the example he set we are clear of the
* charges (?) brought against us and those who oppose [15]
us must answer for themselves if they can

Upon this part of the subject the real question is this "What is baptism according to the fair interpretation "of the word of God?"
1. Here we might bring forward the evidence produced by learned men of the primitive meaning of the ~~word~~ term Baptism: it is singular that it should be so often acknowledged to mean immersion; if it should not be
                    cases ~~===~~
immersion in this ~~circumstances~~ | it follows that the proper sense of the word is not applicable in the New Testament and that inspiration has used, in the acscription [sic] of a sacred rite, a word not used in its primary and proper
                              {from}
sense: and yet after the abundant evidence {of } the use of the term in a variety of ways this must be the reference
from the ~~of~~ sprinkling of modern date as Baptism
2. how besides this let us observe that the Jews word used to immersions and had the requisite conveniences; that was not in their minds any opposition to the * right or to the practice as there is in the minds of many now: it was therefore not in their conceptions to mean less by the words they used that their proper signification and the apostles, originally Jews, made a sad mistake if they gave us in their Greek a wrong word.
3. The constant practice of the ancient church, that part of it particularly which spoke the Greek language and who of course would understand it ~~and~~ better than we can do, shews completely how they understood the terms respecting baptism and whoever has been attended to their writings Even in a general way must come to these conclusions either that they did not understand their

[p. 5]
[[Cont^d
    own language or that the intention of the term Baptism is immersion
4. The provision made for such an administration (?) in the ancient places {?} of Christian worship {?} the change
- - - - - of means from the large Baptistry to the little
~~small~~ font is noticed by learned antiquarians who are

not at all inclined to our views as an Evidence of what
was the ~~case~~ (?) practice in former days
5. The reproaches both of the Jews and the Heathens
cast upon the Christians for their profession of Christ by [10]
their Baptism shew that their Baptisms were immersions
6. The powerful evidence of the acknowledgements of
those who not belonging to us but in fact opponents to our
views yet confess that the baptism of the Lord and the
apostles and the primitive Christians were immersions [15]
    If then the Lord did not mean it to be immersion
why use such terms
II. The second part of our subject is the view given of the
connection between Christ and the Baptized believer "buried
with Christ in baptism." [20]
    When Christ died he was buried; believers in Christ
are often represented as buried with him: that unity between
him and his people is often stated in the writings of Paul
so that they died with him and afterwards rose with him as
if he & they had formed one body and he as a public character [25]
having died in their account they had all died with him &
all rose with him & so were united with him by faith; they
in their baptism declared that this was their profession
& their hope & therefore were buried with Christ in baptism &
were risen with him through faith &c [30]
    It is remarkable also that the apostle uses the same
expression with so slight a variation as to shew that the
idea of being buried was still presented when he said
"buried with him by baptism unto death" Rom: 6. 4.
    This presents a view clear and impressive. your [35]
Baptism is a declaration of your trust in the death of Christ
for life. this trust or rather faith unites us to him; we
are therefore partaker of his death and as a declaration
of it we are baptized in his name. Thus buried with him
by submission to the ordinance which is ~~which is~~ the sign (?) [40]
of his death & burial and using from it as a declaration that
your hope of eternal life and glory is through his
                          {our}
resurrection with whom in the sign of {your} baptism
we use to newness of life

[p. 6]
This view of the subject concedes with all
that occurs in the new Josh[a] on the subject of faith
and baptism; the hope of faith, & the profession of faith
made in baptism

It shews evidently that from these instances
nothing can be concluded respecting circumcision being
designed to stand in the stead of Baptism; it is excluded;
it is the profession of those who believe; it is all the way
through a profession and hope that necessarily supposes
an acquaintance with what the gospel sets before us
and there is, in consequences of this, no instance in which
it is stated to be done with the^view to the a future faith and
hope in Christ which if infants are the subject must be
the object in view: but where does that appear in the
New Testament?

This leads us to advert to the <u>History</u> of
Infant baptism: this is thought to be the strong hold
of the paedobaptists but how little it avails is obvious
to the close inquirer

As there is no instance in the New Testament and
no clear (?) ground <u>upon</u> which it was in that volume (?)
appointed---<u>When</u> it began in the church we know
not: this no proof that it must have been from the
apostles for when infant communion began is equally
unknown & yet now few will say that this practice is
apostolical (?) The first who baptized is admitted to
communion an infant, no one can tell.

But one thing is manifest the first distrust
notice we have of it about the year 200 by Tertullian
supposes it allowable and practiced only in circumstances
of supposed amongst of death.[10]

S[t].. Augustine's mother was a Christian and when
he was an infant & was very ill it was thought he would
die and then there was Her intention of baptizing him; but
he got better and it was then put aside:[11] in the end
he was baptized when grown up to years of maturity[12]

---

[10] See Tertullian (ca.155/160–after 220), *De Baptismo*, 18.

[11] Augustine, *Confessions* 1.11.17.

[12] Augustine, *Confessions* 9.6.14.

{c---------}
In {cases (?) ---} of Infancy sponsors were
introduced who answered for the future faith of the
child: an absurdity in all its bearings.--In the fact
notices we have of the baptism of infants. this practice [40]
is mentioned with disapprobation; the passage is
remarkable; it runs in these terms

[p. 7]
    Having said that delay rather than haste was [1]
                                "ours"
lest particularly respecting infants | or (?) "little ones", he says
"for what need is there (if there be no necessity) for sponsors
"be brought into danger who themselves by their mortality might
"fail of their promises or might be deceived by the growth (?) [5]
"of an Evil disposition"[13] (that is the child) as I understand
the passage, if the sponsors die and have incurred the a
responsibility which remains unfulfilled; they engaged
that the child believed and they die and he not only did does
not believe but they cannot use the means that should [10]
lead him to believe—or if he should shew a perverse
temper and did not all end to the gospel then the sponsor
engaged for that which he could not perform and asserted
that the child did believe when it proved that he neither
did then nor afterwards believe. This was the absurdity [15]
both of the ancient church and of the modern churches that
use it that the sponsors assert the child (?) <u>does</u> believe &
on their making the assertion the child is baptized when
every body present knows that the infant neither does
believe nor can believe. One thing however is manifest [20]
that while their baptism was on a profession of faith it was
seen that no other ground could be tenable.
    The fact appears to be—It was supposed that
Baptism insured salvation and that therefore when the
Infant was in danger this was * considered (?) of vast [25]
important consequence. Whereas the salvation of infants
is never represented as depending either on Baptism or (?)
any other external rite; and while are doubt not they are
saved if they die in infancy, it is evident however that

---

[13] "quid enim necesse, si non tam necesse est, sponsores etiam periculo ingeri, qui et ipsi per mortalitatem destituere promissiones suas possunt et proventu malae indolis falli?" (Tertullian, *Baptismo*, 18.4).

they are not saved by their faith but by another way
The Declarations "He that believes shall be saved"[14] which are
repeated in various forms, belongs not to infants but to
those who are capable of understanding what the will
of the Lord is. That it is a different thing when we
make the appeal th to those that do hope for the
salvation that is in child: to them when not baptized we
boldly say "why sorry ye? did the Lord appoint the
institution to be neglected? does it continue in authority?
why is it neglected? this brings the matter home.

But some will say "What end does it cause so?"
we reply as much as formerly, it was then the declaration
of faith in Christ; it is the same still: it was then the evid^{ce}..
of your submission to the authority of the Lord and of your
source of the excellency of his character, it is the same
still; it was then a declaration of your leaving the

[p. 8]
system of the world for the gospel of Christ; it is the
same still and those who have in sincerity of heart gone
in this road can all testify that its operation on
their minds was altogether that which led them both
to feel their gratitude and their obligation to him
that died for them and rose again
1. But what will the world say? look at the
time when the apostles and the primitive Christians lived
2. What will friends say of me? oh: what did the
Lord say (concerning Father and mother)?[15] Oh!
remember, the question is, what will God say? What
will Christ say?
3. One question more what will you say of it under
other circumstances, in the prospect of going out
of the world without obedience to one (?) part of
the will of Christ? you hope for his salvation
are you doing his will? Some of you are obliged
to answer, No.

NB. there are several arbitrary characters which

---

[14] See Mark 16:16.

[15] See Matthew 10:37; 19:29.

I have forgotten but which by reference to one
or other of the books you will easily decypher
e.g. [two shorthand notes] there are some others which I
do not feel satisfied about; they are all queried
in the margin.

Book Reviews

Matthew C. Bingham, Chris Caughey, R. Scott Clark, Crawford Gribben, and D.G. Hart, *On Being Reformed: Debates over a Theological Identity*. Christianity in the Trans-Atlantic World (Cham, Switzerland: Palgrave Pivot, 2018), vii + 94 pages.

With the recent trendiness associated with being *Reformed*, one has to critically assess this term and ask who can rightfully claim it as their own. In this work, five different authors address this issue, presenting different perspectives on who can identify with this term; throughout, specific attention is given to the question of credibility for the title of "Reformed Baptist."

Chris Caughey and Crawford Gribben argue in chapter one that, since everyone deviates from the original Reformed confessions in some way, no one group has the sole claim on the title "Reformed." On the contrary, the term "Reformed" can be used by any who wish to self-identify as such. According to the authors, however, the problem with this is that the title is used by such a variety of people to mean a variety of things that it has ultimately become irrelevant in offering any sort of helpful identity marker.

The second chapter is by Matthew C. Bingham, who claims that it is appropriate to use the term "Reformed Baptist" when properly defined. He states that although this term is certainly anachronistic as the early Baptists did not identify as Reformed, it is nevertheless helpful for the contemporary church and should thus not be considered an oxymoron. Nevertheless, Bingham describes Reformed Baptists as needing to hold to the Reformed beliefs, such as embracing "the Lord's Day as the Christian Sabbath" and understanding "all of Scripture as covenantally structured" (p. 48). To simply hold to a Calvinistic soteriology is not grounds enough for being considered "Reformed;" one also needs to endorse such aforementioned convictions.

In chapter three, D.G. Hart disagrees with Bingham, claiming that Reformed Protestants are different from Baptists. He aims to show that while Presbyterians desired to stay as close to the Westminster Confession as possible, the Baptists decided to make a new confession that deviated from Westminster beyond the topic of baptism. For this reason—along with a history of divide between Baptists and Presbyterians—Hart argues for a narrower definition of being "Reformed" that does not include Baptists.

The final chapter is by R. Scott Clark, who looks to address the arguments by Gribben, Caughey, and Bingham. Clark attempts to dismantle both arguments and concludes along similar lines as Hart. In the end, Clark believes in the importance of having and defending a clearly defined understanding of "Reformed," one which excludes those who deviate from the system of doctrines set by the early Reformed confessions.

With the intentional brevity of the works in this series, the limitation on the word count of this book can make it seem abrupt. Other than a brief abstract for the series, the book opens with the first chapter and the reader can thus feel thrown into the discussion without any clear overview for the debate being addressed. With this in mind, the book would have benefited from an editor who could have added both an introduction and conclusion to frame the discussion. It would have also been helpful if the chapters each followed a similar structure that addressed similar questions and issues. As it is, one can feel like the authors at times do not properly address each other, and at other moments spend unneeded time in summarizing the views of the chapters that one had just read. An example of the former is seen in a blatant error in Clark's chapter, where he claims that Bingham argues that "it is neither anachronistic nor oxymoronic to speak of Reformed Baptists" (p. 74). Yet Bingham is abundantly clear that "the term 'Reformed Baptist' carries with it a strong sense of anachronism and should not be used to describe early modern actors" (p. 35). With this being such a large part of Bingham's chapter, one hopes Clark simply miswrote. But either way, such an oversight is evidence of a lack of editing put into the final compilation. An editor who could have helped address such deficits would have aided in the readability and cohesion of this volume.

Yet, despite its flaws, this book is a helpful introduction for any who are interested in the potential historical and theological implications of identifying as "Reformed." And for the readership of this journal, it may be of special interest for those who consider themselves to be "Reformed Baptists."

Jonathan N. Cleland
PhD Student, Knox College, University of Toronto
Toronto, Ontario, Canada

Robert G. Ingram, *Reformation without End: Religion, Politics, and the Past in Post-Revolutionary England*, Politics, Culture, and Society in Early Modern Britain (Manchester, England: Manchester University Press, 2018), xx + 362 pages.

This work presents the case that for the English divines of the first half of the eighteenth century, primitive church history served to adjudicate theological disputes that lingered since the Reformation. In *Reformation without End*, Robert Ingram, Professor of History at Ohio University, follows a "polemical war told from four proximate, yet distinct vantages" (p. 6). The author surveys the polemical pamphleteering of Daniel Waterland (1683–1750), Conyers Middleton (1683–1750), Zachary Grey (1688–1766), and William Warburton (1698–1779), whose lives intersected in various ways during the long English Reformation (1660–1832).

The volume is presented in four parts. The initial chapter of each part portrays the life and something of the context of one figure before delving into their respective polemical works in three subsequent chapters each. The polemical careers of each divine demonstrate the way in which eighteenth-century churchmen consciously depended on primitive Christian sources as a standard of orthodoxy and then marshalled those sources for their contemporary aims. Given the emergence of a deistic impulse with natural theology, through works such as Matthew Tindal's (1657–1733) *Christianity as Old as the Creation* (1730) and the counter-methods of weighing truth claims stemming from John Locke (1632–1704) and Isaac Newton (1643–1727), the book hovers around the intersection of reason and revelation. Ingram demonstrates that each figure surveyed was concerned to arrive at truth in a methodologically sound manner for the sake of maintaining orthodoxy in the established church. During this period especially, suspicion of heterodoxy could hinder one's prospects of preferment for improvement of post. When subjects as basic as the divinity of Christ were sometimes in question, landing on the wrong side of a polemical match could prove maddening and even career ending.

While not all of the divines surveyed by the author may be familiar (e.g., Zachary Grey), the author helpfully presents each figure's web of theological allies and polemical opponents so as to provide historical context. All of the figures but Middleton were considered orthodox in their lifetimes. While Waterland and Middleton surpass the others in academic training, Grey's historical acumen and Warburton's clarity of writing on the relation of church and state in England proved notable to the establishment at the time. While all four polemicists considered the best methods of evaluating evidence for miracles through the use of historical sources, each contended for other loci of doctrine as well.

The author contributes to the scholarship of the period in at least two important ways. First, he demonstrates that despite the orthodox preoccupation with natural theology and deistic arguments, polemical divines were also concerned with defending the orthodoxy of the established church from various sides, including Dissenters and Roman Catholics. Second, the author continually reveals the explicit way in which orthodox divines knew, studied, appreciated, and relied on documents from the primitive church. Indeed, some linked Constantine to William Laud, Donatism to Methodism, persecution to the Puritans and Catholics, and the Athanasian Creed to the role of saints and angels in the Christian life.

The scope of the work is vast, the sources expansive, the writing style engaging. The chapters are useful and sensible as standalone essays, but together, they unfold a more thorough picture of each divine. Besides a brief underdeveloped case that Waterland and Grey taught human ability to "earn [and "contribute to"] his or her own salvation" (pp. 253–55), the arguments presented are thorough and sound.

Ingram highlights a relevant feature of polemical dialogue: the tendency to punish, coerce, and stoop to caustic rhetoric. Observing this tendency throughout the chapters (along with Ingram's primary thesis regarding the intersection of revelation, reason, and history) makes the work a significant contribution to the historiography of the period. But further, Ingram's work carries valuable lessons for historians, theologians, and philosophers who traffic in ideas.

Dallas W. Vandiver
PhD, The Southern Baptist Theological Seminary
Louisville, KY

Dennis C. Bustin and Barry H. Howson, *Zealous for the Lord: The Life and Thought of the Seventeenth Century Baptist Hanserd Knollys*, Monographs in Baptist History (Eugene, OR: Pickwick Publications, 2019), x + 132 pages.

Barry H. Howson, ed., *Christ Exalted: Pastoral Writings of Hanserd Knollys with an Essay on his Eschatological Thought*, Monographs in Baptist History, vol. 12 (Eugene, OR: Pickwick Publications, 2019), x + 260 pages.

Due to the fact that we so easily approve products of our own environment, it is good for us to hear voices from other times and places. These jar us out of our own causal assumptions and prompt us to consider again some of the things that we so easily take for granted. Hanserd Knollys (1609–1691) raises such a voice. These two volumes allow us to hear him clearly and powerfully.

Knollys's life spanned almost the whole of the turbulent seventeenth century, and reflected that turbulence. Born in Lincolnshire, and educated under Sibbes at Cambridge University, he was ordained as deacon, and then priest, in 1629. Thus entering the ministry, he discovered that he was neither converted to Christ nor called to preach. Counselled by a preacher called John Wheelwright, Knollys agonised over his state until he was both thoroughly converted and genuinely convinced of a call to preach the gospel. This experience powerfully informed both his soteriology and his ecclesiology, and manifested itself in his ministry. Persecution led to a journey to New England in 1638, but trouble in the new world and family issues in the old brought him home in 1641. His teaching and preaching were interrupted by the outbreak of the Civil War. Knollys's convictions were hardening into those of a persuaded Particular Baptist. He was in contact and varying degrees of conflict with Levellers, Fifth Monarchists, and Quakers, through the war and into the Commonwealth period. The last three decades of his life, from the Restoration to his death, were more marked by persecution and peril than by any outward peace. Many of his writings (six separate volumes) through this period were marked by eschatological concerns; others focused on aspects of church life. He continued to be active in the wider life of the Particular Baptist churches, attending the General Assemblies of 1690 and 1691, before the Lord called him home on September 19, 1691. He was buried in Bunhill Fields.

This life is laid out in rich detail and with helpful analysis in Bustin and Howson's *Zealous for the Lord*. They trace the development and expression of the man's convictions over eight chapters. The first five are primarily a chronological survey, while the latter three are more topical—one's focuses on Christian life, the church, and ministry, one on eschatology, and the last provides several lessons to be learned from Knollys's life.

It is these thematic concerns which are the primary focus of the second book under consideration, *Christ Exalted*. This collection of certain published writings begins with Knollys's fascinating autobiography, incomplete in the sense that it concludes in 1672. There are also sermons, each—like the autobiography—preceded by a useful introduction and breakdown of the sermonic structure: three on *Christ Exalted* (1645–1646) from Colossians 3:12, Luke 19:10, and Ephesians 1:4; one on Matthew 25:1–13, *The Parable of the Kingdom of God Expounded* (1674); and, one addressing unfulfilled prophecies, entitled *The World that Now is and the World that Is to Come* (1681). The whole concludes with another survey of Knollys's eschatological thought (remarkable not least for the fact that the footnotes, taken altogether, may be longer than the actual essay). The similarly-titled material on eschatology in *Zealous for the*

Lord is topical, focusing on various ideas that repeatedly crop up in Knollys's writings. This one is tied particularly to Knollys's commentary on Revelation. In fact, these essays are helpful as a way of situating oneself with regard to Knollys's thought before reading the sermons themselves.

This collection pulls us in various directions. On the one hand, we see something of Knollys's typical Puritanism in all its spiritual vigour: he is a preacher of righteousness determined to set life and death before his hearers, pointing them to Christ and pleading with them to close with him in faith, and to walk in genuine newness of life. Any preacher might learn much from the substance of Knollys's preaching here, its earnest tones and gospel clarity. We might not model ourselves on his structures, but his style—the way he handles his text, the way he presses home the truth—is stirring. On the other hand, there is also the concern (nearly an obsession, typical of the milieu within which Knollys operated) with the details of the last days. For most Particular Baptists today, Knollys shows a staggering over-confidence in identifying the specifics of the end of all things: signs, times, places, events and periods. He was a robust post-millennial, anticipating a literal thousand-year reign of Christ with his saints on earth—the latter-day glory of the Saviour's spiritual return—followed by a physical return and the establishment of the eternal kingdom. To read Knollys handling Scriptures to prove these points is to enter a hermeneutical realm that may be foreign to many and strangely familiar to some. He actually outlived his predicted world's end (about 1688) by some three years. One wonders how a godly man of genuine conviction handles such a turn of events! These really are fascinating sermons, and one feels the compelling power of a persuaded personality pleading for deeply-felt realities of present and eternal consequence.

What, then, do we make of the life and the labours as presented here? Do we read him as an oddity, more distant in faith and life than particularly helpful? Do we dismiss him because of some of his exegetical flights, or embrace him because he proves a point?

Knollys may not be first in the galaxy of seventeenth-century Particular Baptists, but there is much about him that is typical of them and useful for us. His pastoral priorities come quickly to the fore. His zeal for souls seems indicative of the spirit of the Particular Baptists during their period of stunning expansion. In both books, in different ways, we get glimpses into the Calvinistic soteriology of the early Baptists, and how it was derived both from a study of Scripture and their own experience of grace; we see the concern for practical godliness in every sphere of a believer's life; we note how such persuasion informs and is informed by their crisp and vigorous doctrine of the church and its ordinances.

At the same time, Knollys challenges some of our neat categorisations. He had a reputation as a man whose prayers for divine healing were often and notably heard on high, though he always ascribed the power and the glory to God. Might some rear back at this? His strong insistence both on free grace in conversion and the necessity of holiness in a convert will keep us from the errors of our own times. His fascination with eschatology might trouble us, but—as those living through turbulent times ourselves—might at least provoke us to consider whether or not we give sufficient attention to the last things, pressing both believers and unbelievers to look beyond this present world to the world which is to come, and to live accordingly (even if we might resist the temptation to absolute specificity which Knollys sometimes indulged).

Zealous for the Lord is probably a better introduction to the man himself, and a grand example of a careful, thorough and accessible survey of such a life. The concluding remarks to the earlier chapters keep us focused on the main issues of Knollys's life, and the latter chapters show us some of the concerns which captured his heart. The final chapter presenting lessons keeps Knollys from lying on the page; he leaps off it and grabs us by the scruff of the neck and makes us think about things. *Christ Exalted* lets us listen to the man himself, and it is easy to catch the tones not of a polemicist and provocateur, but of a real pastor-preacher. As such, these sermons study us at least as much as we might study them.

I therefore hope that a good number will hear the voice of Hanserd Knollys sounding from these pages, and that he will go on jarring us out of grooves and ruts, and challenge us to consider whether or not we, in our generation, serve the risen and reigning Christ with the same fervour and vigour that Knollys displayed in his.

Jeremy Walker
Pastor, Maidenbower Baptist Church
Crawley, England

Michael Davies and W.R. Owen, ed., *The Oxford Handbook of John Bunyan* (Oxford: Oxford University Press, 2018), xxviii + 681 pages.

There can be no doubting the worth of this remarkable collection of essays on all things Bunyan. It is a celebration of the last fruitful few decades in which Bunyan Studies has come into its own. This is also a monumental work: nearly seven-hundred pages long; structured with elegant coherence in four parts; comprising no less than 38 essays plus an introduction; and including the mature work of so many capable scholars at the top of their game. The sheer magnitude of the volume, together with the vision, labour and ambition of the editors, is impressive.

The first part, "Contexts," places Bunyan within his world. There are essays on the wider context of Dissent, Bunyan's Bedford congregation, his relationship with the Bible and with writing, writers and printers. Perhaps readers of this journal may be most interested in Dewey D. Wallace's typically accomplished essay on Bunyan's theology and religious context. He presents Bunyan's moderate Calvinism as "a theology of comfort and intended for the comfort of others who felt themselves hopelessly lost souls" (p. 70). Michael Davies' Introduction also wrestles sympathetically with how Bunyan's theology may be the one aspect of his literary and historical standing that causes most "difficulty" for many modern readers and scholars (p. 6).

Part two, "Works," is a blend of two types of essays. One type focuses on different periods in Bunyan's literary career and on his poetry. The other type focuses on particular works: Bunyan's biography, *Grace Abounding to the Chief of Sinners*; *The Pilgrim's Progress* (with an essay on each of the first and second instalments); *The Life and Death of Mr Badman*; and *The Holy War*. One essay stands out in particular, for me at least. Michael Davies' essay on *The Pilgrim's Progress*, such an important much-worked-over text, is sublime. He describes Bunyan's most influential work as "a scriptural art": "we are taken not just through a tale of spiritual progress, an *ordo salutis* that traces the stages of conversion from conviction of sin to perseverance in faith—an allegorical version, that is, of Bunyan's *Grace Abounding*—but also through the pages of the Bible" (p. 247).

The third part picks up on "Directions in Criticism," with a broad range of essays from emblem and allegory to "Prison and the Place of Creativity" to poststructuralism and postmodernism and on to post-secular criticism. The risk of a volume this size is that the wide variety of subjects and authors leads to fragmentation. The editors and contributors have successfully avoided that danger. The coherence of the whole project shows its worth in this section where the earlier engagement with Bunyan's world and works weaves its way into this more theoretical and critical assessment of his literary achievement. To return to *The Pilgrim's Progress*, Julie Coleman's essay reflects on Bunyan's "linguistic artistry" and "artful simplicity" (p. 413), even his Puritan simplicity. She demonstrates how the rich imaginative energy of the work rests on a relatively small number of root words, most of them monosyllabic. Thus in *The Pilgrim's Progress* Bunyan presented his theological vision in the most accessible way possible, not just in form of the work (as a story, or a dream) but also in the deliberate deployment of its vocabulary. In his hands, simple words have great power.

The final part of the volume focuses is an exercise in reception history. Various essays reflect on Bunyan's influence in different periods and around the globe, on children as well as adults. To return to *The Pilgrim's Progress* once more, Nathalie Collé contributes an essay on the illustrations, visual representations, and "extra-textual paraphernalia" (p. 648) of that enduring work in many different forms. Isabel Rivers examines the way in which all sorts of groups within the eighteenth-century Evangelical Revival made extensive use of *The Pilgrim's Progress* as one of their most revered texts, sometimes for polemical purposes but more importantly to build the faith of believers whether in families, small groups, or congregations.

It is impossible in a short review to do justice to the rich scholarship in this volume of essays. For any reader daunted by its sheer size, there is the pleasure of picking and choosing from among the many topics on offer. There is surely something of interest for everyone, either opening up new dimensions or covering familiar ground with fresh insight. I am particularly interested in personality, and I might have hoped for an essay on Bunyan's personality—surely a topic with rich material to work with. I felt at times, particularly in that first part, that we were learning a great deal about everything around the man, but not so much about the man himself. Even so, I can hardly quibble at the omission of what would have been the 39th essay, and the cumulative weight of the volume builds up an impressively clear picture of this important writer, leader and theologian.

Tim Cooper
Associate Professor and Head of the School of Arts
University of Otago, Dunedin, New Zealand

Michael A.G. Haykin and Brian Croft with Ian H. Clary, *Being a Pastor: A Conversation with Andrew Fuller* (Darlington, Durham: EP Books, 2019), 256 pages.

Ours is a day in which pragmatism and personality leadership plague the church. Church metrics focus on growth in numbers and platforms of influence outside of the local church as measures of health. The result is a continual ebb and flow of gimmicks and gurus, in reality, a lot of silliness. Or worse, in some cases, pastors that Paul would identify as promoting themselves (2 Cor 10:12), preaching for profit (2 Cor 2:17), and tickling worldly ears (2 Tim 4:3). The solution? Step one, return to the Scriptures for clarity on who pastors are supposed to be and what they are supposed to do. Step two, look at the history of the church for faithful examples to learn from and emulate.

Michael A.G. Haykin and Brian Croft hold up Andrew Fuller (1754–1815), the English Particular Baptist minister, theologian, and early champion of the modern mission's movement, as one such faithful example of pastoral ministry. They see their exercise as one of "pastoral *ressourcement*, in which Fuller's thinking about and practice of pastoral ministry is shown to be quite germane for modern-day ministers and congregations" (p. 20). Their efforts ably accomplish this purpose in three main sections.

In section one, Haykin offers two chapters providing the historical and theological context. The first is a survey of ordination sermons among the eighteenth-century English Dissenters. The dissenting community was made up of the denominations outside the established Church of England, primarily Presbyterians, Baptists, and Independents, also known as Congregationalists. When pastors were ordained in these traditions, the ordination service included a sermon exhorting the ordinands and often a charge to the local congregation. This makes these sermons a wealth of information about how the pastoral office was conceived and its duties discharged. Haykin unpacks one of these sermons from Matthew Henry (Presbyterian, 1662–1714), John Gill (Baptist, 1697–1771), and Philip Doddridge (Independent, 1702–1751) respectively to show that Fuller was in good company with his pastoral priorities.

The second chapter is an exposition of one of Fuller's own ordination sermons. The elevated role of preaching has been well documented in the past. Haykin's contribution here is highlighting the emphasis on character as integral to pastoral ministry. The pastor is to be a good man, as demonstrated in the home and in public. His spiritual vitality is to be founded upon the Word and fueled by prayer. And he is to be a man anointed by the Spirit of God. In Fuller's words, "eminent spirituality in a minister is usually attended with eminent usefulness" (p. 79).

Part two contains the seventeen extant sermons of Fuller to ordinands, plus two addresses to Baptist academies, all freshly edited by Haykin. In these sermons, "Fuller lays out what is essentially a manual of pastoralia" (p. 23). What the reader will find in this "manual," is the advice and wisdom of a seasoned pastor, majoring on the two great themes of the pastor's life and the ministry of the Word. One illustration of this characteristic wedding of life and public ministry, from his sermon on Titus 2:15:

> Beware that you do not preach an unfelt Gospel. If you do, it will be seen, and you will be despised. It will be seen that, though you affect to be in earnest, you do not feel; and that you scarcely believe your own doctrine. We may get into the habit of talking for the truth, and pleading for holiness, and yet be dead ourselves; and if so, we shall be sure to be despised (p. 135).

In part three, Croft elevates Fuller as a timeless solution to questions that swirl around pastoral ministry. In the current environment, what Croft terms an evangelical crisis, Fuller serves as an antidote to both pragmatism and personality leadership. These twin, contemporary aberrations are wreaking havoc on the church in America. One of the many tragic effects of these leadership models is the current rate of pastoral fallout. Fuller is a welcome reminder that being a faithful pastor means watching over oneself and one's flock. From Fuller's personal example, Croft exhorts pastors to understand their call, strive for usefulness, cultivate their affections, pursue faithfulness, and focus on Christ. From Fuller's pastoral theology, he calls pastors to preach the Word, care for souls, shepherd your sheep, be a godly example, and prioritize their families. Poignantly, in Fuller's words, "Hundreds of ministers have been ruined by indulging a thirst for the character of a *great* man, while they have neglected the far superior character of the *good* man" (p. 70).

From the title of the book, *Being a Pastor: A Conversation with Andrew Fuller*, it is not exactly clear that the majority of its content is actually edited primary source material. But this becomes clear, and overall this addition to Andrew Fuller studies is welcome. Due to the significance of the ordination sermon as a genre for the understanding of pastoral theology, Haykin and Croft's work will be of interest to those studying what historians call the "long eighteenth century." Beyond this, however, and more to the authors' purpose, the book is helpful for pastors, either as encouragement or correction. But it would also be useful to all Christians in evaluating what kind of ministry to place themselves under for pastoral care.

Andrew S. Ballitch
Associate Pastor of Preaching and Ministries
Westwood Alliance Church, Mansfield, OH

Andrew Fuller, *The Life of Samuel Pearce*, Foreword by Michael A.G. Haykin (Peterborough, ON: H&E Publishing, 2020), ix + 184 pages.

A year before Samuel Pearce's (1766–1799) call to minister the congregation of Canon Street in Birmingham, he received a request from his seminary friend Joseph Kinghorn (1766–1832) on the marble trade in Plymouth. However, Pearce did not reply to Kinghorn until a few months later. In the letter, dated July 17, 1788, Pearce apologised for his inattentiveness and explained:

Picture to yourself, my dear Kinghorn, your friend Pearce arriving home on Saturday night, scarce having time to look about him, before fatigue called him to the arms of Morpheus, rising early the following day, preparing for three public exercises, and from that time to the present, in the midst of a numerous acquaintance, engaging constantly four, five, or six times every week, in the old trade of preaching and attendance on prayer and society meetings, to which both duty and delight solicited his presence—and say, is it surprising if amidst so much animation, inanimate marble should escape his notice?

Pearce's apology reveals his charitable character and life as a gospel minister. For all those who knew Pearce, he was "eminently distinguished by the suavity of temper, the gentleness of manner, and the sweetness of aspect" (Martin Hood Wilkin, *Joseph Kinghorn, of Norwich* [1855], p. 125). With his extended reputation among both Baptists and broader evangelicals, the "seraphic" Samuel Pearce was certainly not a product of Andrew Fuller's memoir. Instead, with Pearce's extraordinary love for God and men, Fuller felt it is worthy for his and later generations to learn from his dear friend. As both Peter J. Morden and Michael A.G. Haykin pointed out, Fuller saw Pearce as a model of evangelical Calvinistic spirituality and a true missionary. Therefore, like earlier Christian biographies, such as Athanasius' (ca. 296/8–373) *Life of Anthony* and Jonathan Edwards' (1703–1758) *Life of David Brainerd*, Fuller's *Memoirs of the Rev. Samuel Pearce* is more than a chronicle; instead, it reveals the heart and mechanism of Fullerism.

During Fuller's lifetime, the *Memoirs* was revised three times (1800, 1801, 1808), and later it was reprinted more than thirty times in both Britain and America. Despite his popularity in the nineteenth century, Samuel Pearce was by and large forgotten by many Baptists in the twentieth century. Consequently, Fuller's *Memoirs* was buried in dust along with other spiritual treasures. Though in the previous generation, both S. Pearce Carey (1862–1953) and Ernest A. Payne (1902–1980) significantly contributed to the studies of Pearce's life, they did not see the need to reprint Fuller's biography of Pearce. Much like how J.I. Packer discovered and made John Owen (1616–1683) accessible in the mid-twentieth century, Michael Haykin began to write and teach about Pearce from the 1980s onwards. With Haykin's efforts and influence, Solid Ground Christian Books reprinted Fuller's *Memoirs* in 2005, under the title *A Heart for Missions: Memoir of Samuel Pearce*. This modern printing is based on the third edition of the *Memoirs* (1808), and it is the first attempt to publish it as a single, separate, and readable volume. After more than thirty years of research, Haykin edited and published a critical edition of the *Memoirs*, which is the fourth volume of *The Complete Works of Andrew Fuller*, published by Walter De Gruyter. With an extended introduction, Haykin used the 1808 edition as the basis and indicated any differences from the previous two editions in the footnotes.

Unlike these two modern printings, the current volume, published by the Hesed and Emet Publishing House, specifically aims to broaden the *Memoirs*' contemporary readership. As the publisher noticed, "in this edition, the punctuation and capitalization have been modernized, some archaic words have been updated, and a few other slight editorial changes made" (p. iv). To aid their contemporary readers, the editors shortened each chapter's title and inserted subtitles before each section. In addition to the *Memoirs*, the editors also included six of Pearce's hymns, a list of recommended readings on Fuller, and an index of scriptures. With its simple layout and eloquent fonts, readers will find this volume incredibly readable. Thus, this is a friendly introduction to not only the life of Samuel Pearce but also to Fullerism. As there are many different spiritualties available on the market today, this volume is most needed for evangelicals to recover a Bible-guided and Christocentric spirituality.

However, due to their commitment to readability, the editors deliberately abandoned Fuller's original footnotes and only indicated biblical and other necessary references. Besides, the editors refined original correspondence quotations. By merging or dividing original paragraphs, the editors also excluded some parts of a letter. For instance, in Pearce's letter, dated August 15, 1792 (p. 7), the editors merged the first two paragraphs and left out the following sentences: "You have no doubt perused Mr. Ryland's letter to me, wherein I find he solicits an exchange. The reason he assigns is so obviously important, that a much greater sacrifice than we are called to make should not be withheld to accomplish it. I therefore propose, God willing, to spend the next Lord's day at Northampton. I thought of taking tea with you this evening: that would have been highly gratifying to us both; but it must be our meat and dream to do and submit to the will of our heavenly Father." A similar example is found in Pearce's letter to William Steadman (1765–1837) on February 8, 1793 (pp. 24–25). The editors cut out the final paragraph, where Pearce wrote: "We shall be glad of all your assistance in a pecuniary way, as the expense will be heavy. Dear brother Carey has paid us a visit of love this week. He preached excellently tonight. I expect brother Thomas next week, or the week after. I wish you would meet him here. I have a house at your command, and a heart greatly attached to you." Though with good intentions, the editors should admit and indicate this kind of content changes, as it cannot be qualified as "slight" changes in nature. If the editors decide to revise this contemporary edition, they shall consider to include a biographical glossary, where readers can have a brief introduction to the lives of people like Steadman, Fuller, or William Carey (1761–1834).

Overall, evangelical ministers and churchmen will appreciate the contemporary edition of Fuller's *Memoirs of the Rev. Samuel Pearce*, published by the

Hesed and Emet Publishing House. With its simplicity and readability, many will rediscover the exemplary life of Samuel Pearce and the spirituality of Fullerism, through this edition. As Michael Haykin remarked in his introduction, "I could say much more, but I hope that this more than suffices to whet the reader's appetite for Fuller's remarkable memoir of his friend that proved to be the most popular of all his many books" (p. ix).

Baiyu Andrew Song
PhD cand., The Southern Baptist Theological Seminary
Louisville, KY

Matthew Bingham, *Orthodox Radicals: Baptist Identity in the English Revolution* (Oxford: Oxford University Press, 2019), xi + 146 pages.

In light of the strong thesis, it is surprising that the author, Matthew Bingham, in the title includes the words "Baptist Identity." That is the very point of historiographical contention, a nomenclature that is fallacious in the time under consideration. The book's thesis, stated early and reiterated throughout, is applied consistently to every part of the argument. His closing summation of chapter five states it well: "Despite the contrary suggestions of some historians, those who rejected paedobaptism were not driven by a unique or distinctively 'Baptist' vision, hermeneutic or way of reading scripture. Rather, they were participating in a broader religious culture and simply pressed the logic of certain widely-shared assumptions further than most of their contemporaries were willing to do" (p. 145). Again in the last sentence of chapter 5 he succinctly summarized his driving concern. To grasp a better sense of the self-understanding of these developing churches we must think "in terms of baptistic congregations and individuals questioning paedobaptism, but not lapsing into denominational labels derived from later decades." These labels "fabricate a co-ordinated, self-aware religious group that did not exist," and make us unaware of "the rather more subtle range of religious self-identities that were actually emerging during the period" (p. 146).

The author develops this thesis in five chapters plus an introduction and conclusion. In chapter one he investigates the "Jessey circle" out of which the first Calvinistic "baptistic congregationalists" (his preferred nomenclature) arose. Chapter two analyzes the self-identity of those who signed the 1644/1646 confessions and re-evaluates the term "Particular Baptist" assigned them by historians. Chapter three argues that a commonly shared congregational ecclesiology made the "rejection of paedobaptism a viable, mainstream, intellectual possibility for the first time in England's history" (p. 62). Chapter four looks at baptistic congregationalists during the Cromwellian period, employing his nuanced framework of discussion better to understand both the extent and the shape of religious liberty granted during the interregnum. Chapter five examines the interrelationships between the "ecumenical" minded baptistic congregationalists and the "sectarian" baptistic congregationalists. The conclusion applies Bingham's thesis to selected literature arguing for its positive affect to correct the "widespread historiographical assumption that one can appropriately and coherently describe a distinctive 'Baptist' identity during the English Revolution and Interregnum." (p. 147).

Bingham's knowledge and pertinent use of both primary and secondary source material is impressive. In the space of 157 pages he includes 649 footnotes. He ties together sources and personal narrative in an artistic way carefully constructing his argument with literary grace.

I mention three caveats. One is his contention that a false historiography is generated by using the word "Baptist" as a denominational label. Some of the baptistic congregationalists were hesitant to embrace the truly differentiating power resident within their rejection of pedobaptism. They had initiated, nevertheless, an ecclesiological option entirely distinct from the pedobaptistic congregationalism within which they continued to operate for a brief period. Their distinct ecclesiology would soon be known as "Baptist." It was probably the single most significant ecclesiological insight of the seventeenth century—far beyond the congregational polity to which separatism gave rise. Using the word does not change the substance of their ecclesiology. Nor does its use as convenient nomenclature compromise the historiographical integrity of invested scholars.

Another: It is true that there is an organic theological continuity between congregationalism and believers' baptism. A purely congregational polity cannot be maintained with constant adding of the unregenerate through infant baptism. Theological continuity is important, but the constant energy throughout the ecclesiological pilgrimage is the Reformation principle of *sola scriptura*. Bingham does point to this but argues that the baptism move was only intellectually feasible within the preceding congregational context. Maybe; but the rise of the Swiss Anabaptists could offer an alternative way of looking at that connection with an emphasis on "Truth is immortal."

Finally, throughout his analysis, the author reiterates the difficulty of sustaining "the suggestion that believer's baptism was, in and of itself, constitutive of a new, coherent, and historiographically meaningful self-identity." The baptistic congregationalists viewed pedobaptism, so the author claims, "as simply one more 'popish' barnacle that had inappropriately attached itself to the ark of Christ's church" (p. 136). Its removal, therefore, so they surmised, "would not have necessarily required the creation of a new 'Baptist' self-identity built around a new understanding of the sacrament." (p. 136 *et passim*). For a relatively small group, perhaps, this was true, but it also was true that many realized virtually immediately that the removal of this barnacle changed everything. That was the chief element uniting church and state, thus infringing on liberty of conscience, and maintaining the clearly open bridge between the church and the world. It took a while for the distinctiveness of the word "Baptist" to denote a specific identifiable ecclesiological option, but the reality was present with full implications of liberty of conscience, separation of church and state, and church discipline when that step was taken. The mere triviality of how long before a specific nomenclature began to be used to identify this group does not diminish the reality that pedobaptist congregationalists and baptistic congregationalists could not long co-exist in the same ecclesiological structure. Nor does it justify the persistent criticism of historians for employing the word "Baptist" when they investigate these phenomena. The "Baptist" movement had really and truly begun. Baptism sealed the covenant and was the door to enjoying all other gospel privileges together as a church. Spilsbery argued this without equivocation. The author looks at this important point in the life of Edward Terrill and concludes with significant profundity, "These peculiarities raised the stakes of baptismal disagreement and ensured that believers-only baptism would function as a catalyst for radicalization among otherwise like-minded congregationalists" (p. 139).

Tom J. Nettles
Senior Professor of Historical Theology
The Southern Baptist Theological Seminary

THE T.V. HAYKIN ESSAY PRIZE

The Andrew Fuller Center for Baptist Studies is pleased to announce the launching of a new annual essay competition in memory of Mrs. T.V. Haykin (1933–1976). The T.V. Haykin Essay Prize seeks to recognize and reward outstanding female Christian researchers in Baptist history and thought.

The T.V. Haykin Essay Prize aims to encourage submissions from female graduate and doctoral students from all over the globe and early career researchers who are within five years of obtaining their PhD. The essay will be on any topic related to the English Particular Baptist history and thought in the long eighteenth century (ca.1689–1834). It should be around 5,000 words (including footnotes following the Chicago-Turabian style) in length. The editorial board of *The Journal of Andrew Fuller Studies* will review all submissions to select the T.V. Haykin Essay Prize winner.

The winner will receive:
- Publication of the winning essay in the Journal of Andrew Fuller Studies;
- $500 (Canadian currency) cash award

Competition Rules:
- Entries should be submitted to bsong@heritagecs.edu before November 30, 2021.
- Entries submitted to the T.V. Haykin Essay Prize must not be under consideration for publication elsewhere.
- The winner of the T.V. Haykin Essay Prize will be required to prove their academic status.

CENTER *for* BAPTIST STUDIES
at THE SOUTHERN BAPTIST THEOLOGICAL SEMINARY

CENTER *for* BAPTIST STUDIES
at THE SOUTHERN BAPTIST THEOLOGICAL SEMINARY

The Andrew Fuller Center for Baptist Studies, located at The Southern Baptist Theological Seminary in Louisville, Kentucky, seeks to promote the study of Baptist history as well as theological reflection on the contemporary significance of that history. The center is named in honor of Andrew Fuller (1754–1815), the late eighteenth- and early nineteenth- century English Baptist pastor and theologian, who played a key role in opposing aberrant thought in his day as well as being instrumental in the founding and early years of the Baptist Missionary Society. Fuller was a close friend and theological mentor of William Carey, one of the pioneers of that society.

The Andrew Fuller Center holds an annual two-day conference in September that examines various aspects of Baptist history and thought. It also supports the publication of the critical edition of the Works of Andrew Fuller, and from time to time, other works in Baptist history. The Center seeks to play a role in the mentoring of junior scholars interested in studying Baptist history.

andrewfullercenter.org

DE GRUYTER

The Andrew Fuller Works Project

It is with deep gratitude to God that The Andrew Fuller Center for Baptist Studies announces that the publishing house of Walter de Gruyter, with head offices in Berlin and Boston, has committed itself to the publication of a modern critical edition of the entire corpus of Andrew Fuller's published and unpublished works. Walter de Gruyter has been synonymous with high-quality, landmark publications in both the humanities and sciences for more than 260 years. The preparation of a critical edition of Fuller's works, part of the work of the Andrew Fuller Center, was first envisioned in 2004. It is expected that this edition will comprise twelve to fourteen volumes and take seven or so years to publish.

The importance of the project

The controlling objective of The Works of Andrew Fuller Project is to preserve and accurately transmit the text of Fuller's writings. The editors are committed to the finest scholarly standards for textual transcription, editing, and annotation. Transmitting these texts is a vital task since Fuller's writings, not only for their volume, extent, and scope, but for their enduring importance, are major documents in both the Baptist story and the larger history of British Dissent.

From a merely human perspective, if Fuller's theological works had not been written, William Carey would not have gone to India. Fuller's theology was the mainspring behind the formation and early development of the Baptist Missionary Society, the first foreign missionary society created by the Evangelical Revival of the last half of the eighteenth century and the missionary society under whose auspices Carey went to India. Very soon, other missionary societies were established, and a new era in missions had begun as the Christian faith was increasingly spread outside of the West, to the regions of Africa and Asia. Carey was most visible at the fountainhead of this movement. Fuller, though not so visible, was utterly vital to its genesis.

andrewfullercenter.org/the-andrew-fuller-works-project

H&E Publishing is a Canadian evangelical publishing company located out of Peterborough, Ontario. We exist to provide Christ-exalting, Gospel-centred, and Bible-saturated content aimed to show God to be as glorious and worthy as He truly is.

hesedandemet.com

www.ingramcontent.com/pod-product-compliance
Lightning Source LLC
Chambersburg PA
CBHW030913080526
44589CB00010B/276